D0820288

WORLDS
□APART□

WORLDS ☐APART☐
Segregated Schools in Northern Ireland

Dominic Murray

Appletree Press

for Siobhan, Fergal, Bronagh and Aidan

First published and printed by
The Appletree Press Ltd
7 James Street South
Belfast BT2 8DL
1985

Copyright © Dominic Murray, 1985

9 8 7 6 5 4 3 2 1

*All rights reserved. No part of this
publication may be reproduced, stored in a
retrieval system, or transmitted, in any form
or by any means, electronic, mechanical,
photocopying, recording, or otherwise, without
the prior permission of the copyright owner*

British Library Cataloguing in Publication Data
Murray, Dominic
World's apart: segregated schools in Northern Ireland
1. Elementary school—Northern Ireland
2. Church and education—Northern Ireland
I. Title
372.9416   LA649.N6

ISBN 0-86281-145-7

Contents

Acknowledgements

My very sincere thanks are due to Francis Douglas who laboured through many drafts in search of inaccuracies and glimpses of my Catholic 'slip'. I am indebted also to David Dunlop and Tommy Lockhart who willingly answered my endless questions concerning Protestant culture and perception. Most of all I am deeply grateful to the principals and staff of 'St Judes' and 'Rathlin' who treated me with such consideration and kindness.

Introduction

There are two distinct communities in Northern Ireland, usually described in the religious terms of Roman Catholic and Protestant. Being a member of either community, however, entails much more than simply being of one or other religious persuasion. It involves the possession of values, traditions, beliefs, attitudes and aspirations, all of which contribute to the culture of that community.

While this culture is most often portrayed in religious terms, it should more properly be described as the totality of the inter-relationships and mutual reinforcements of these traditions, histories and customs. Religion then, as just one element, might best be seen as the stamp on a membership card which allows admittance to one or other of the 'cultural clubs', the norms and regulations of which are subsequently determined by traditional and historical considerations. Barritt and Carter (1972) have described these well:

> The Catholic community gathers to itself the memories of an oppressed nation, the pride of a remote Celtic past before the Norman invaders came, the bitterness of a people leaderless and dispossessed at the time of the plantations. The Protestant community has its own proud memories of the struggle for freedom of conscience at Derry and the Boyne, of high principles successfully maintained, of ordered and productive agriculture and industry brought to an undeveloped land and of an ascendency held by constant vigilance, enterprise and hard work.

This, however, is too stark a dichotomy. In the first place it depicts the Protestant community as a homogenous mass, which it certainly is not. In addition it seems to suggest that all Catholics are proud of their Celtic ancestry just as all Protestants cling to the memory of their struggle for religious freedom of conscience at the Boyne, neither of which is invariably true. One can never pontificate when describing the aspirations and attitudes of the two main cultural groups in Northern Ireland; conditional clauses must always be used.

The best chance of comprehension may well be through analogy. If

7

the attractions of being Irish or British can be represented as two magnets acting on the total population in Northern Ireland then, historically, the former magnet has exerted more 'pull' on the Catholic population and the latter has had more attraction for the Protestant community. Behaviour may range from paramilitary action in defence of historical aspirations to a stage where the only manifestations of 'magnetic pull' are, on the one side, almost involuntary feelings of release, or relief, on crossing the border into the Republic or, on the other side, a faint stirring in the breast at the passing of an Orange parade (an annual celebration by Protestant Orangemen commemorating the Battle of the Boyne). Positions in the magnetic field rarely change significantly, since the social network of most of the individuals concerned consists almost entirely of their co-religionists. Perhaps it is because of the difficulty of delineating and distinguishing cultural identities in Northern Ireland that people there have more often tended to attribute various behavioural and attitudinal traits to each group, in the conviction that they are unique to that group:

> . . . The Catholic is a charming and courteous person, open in manner and eloquent in speech. His faults are those of volatility 'easy come, easy go'. 'A glib person,' says the Protestant.

> . . . The Ulster Protestant is a cautious, logical and far-seeing person in speech and action and he distrusts eloquence. His virtue is that of stability. 'A stiff person,' says the Catholic.

> *(W. R. Rodgers, 1974)*

Poets seem to have been absorbed by the problem of cultural identity.

> A long narrow room with four blue statues of
>   the virgin, and silence
> And school boys of another faith and tradition
> sit at desks, with solemn faces,
> And I expressionless, stare at each
> Concious of the bond and break between us.

> *(John Boyd, 1969)*

The poet, a Protestant, is describing a classroom in a Catholic school which, because of its atmosphere, he finds quite alien.

This word 'atmosphere' is often applied to schools within Northern Ireland's segregated system of education. However, segregation tends to be so rigid and exclusive that few, if any, individuals have the opportunity to experience the ethos of schools which serve a culture other than their own.

Representatives of the Roman Catholic Church in particular have publicly and consistently proclaimed the benefits, and indeed necessity, of the unique ethos of their schools. Indeed it is often argued to be a *sine qua non* of Catholic education. However, comment is rarely made on the manifestations of this ethos and, perhaps more importantly, on how it is attained and fostered. It is quite often argued that its very essence lies in the fact that it does not lend itself to quantification.

Such an axiomatic approach to a highly complex issue may well suffice for those directly involved, i.e. Catholics, but it does little to assuage the ignorance, and perhaps suspicion, of those who can only view such establishments from afar. It is highly likely that the Catholic response to this criticism would be that it is not their responsibility to provide an information service. However, in a culturally uncomfortable country several questions immediately arise – is such an ethos confined to the religious domain? Are religion and culture so interwined in Northern Ireland as to ensure that pupils in segregated schools are subjected to one restricted view of both?

This ignorance and suspicion does not exist about Catholic schools only. Perceptions and attitudes confided to me by Catholic teachers during my research often portrayed Protestant schools as bastions of colonialism, establishments where the philosophy of Protestant ascendancy is encouraged and places where anything Irish is treated with scorn. Of crucial importance here is the fact that such perceptions and stereotypes are spawned and articulated in an almost total lack of first-hand knowledge of what actually takes place in the 'alien' schools.

To date, this lack of knowledge has in no way inhibited public debate on segregated schools. In fact it has actually facilitated outrageous statements being made and extreme views being held by critics of each type of school. Even moderate commentators in the debate seem to agree, and indeed take for granted, that there is a real difference in the experiences undergone by Catholic and Protestant children within their denominational schools.

The Roman Catholic case for retaining their schools rests on a conviction that they provide a religio-moral ethos which is central to Catholic education. Those opposed to segregation usually base their case on the belief that separate schools encourage divisiveness by propagating different, and perhaps hostile, cultural heritages. Both these positions are based on the conviction that schools attended by Protestant and Catholic children are significantly different sorts of institutions and that different activities are practised within them.

Indeed this notion underpins almost all discussions and debate about the 'problem' of integrated education. It is quite amazing, therefore, that so little information exists about the segregated schools themselves. There have been a small number of attempts to increase our knowledge about them— Darby (1976); Robinson (1971); Magee (1970); Murray (1978); Hadkins (1971) and Russell (1972)—but although these have been interesting and informative, their findings have generally been made available to a predominantly academic audience and seem to have done little to advance the general debate on integrated education in Northern Ireland beyond mere polemic or ill-informed rhetoric. The stimulus for this book therefore was provided by the wide general interest in integrated education and the distinct lack of knowledge about segregated schools. It represents the result of six years research carried out between 1976 and 1982 involving extensive study of, and within, segregated schools in Northern Ireland.

This background enquiry took two forms. In the first place I was involved in a mainly quantitative study of the degree of religious polarisation in the educational system in Northern Ireland. I also attempted to gather information about the similarities and differences in practice demonstrated by the segregated schools. I studied 152 schools in a questionnaire sample in an attempt to gain a general profile of school practice and procedure. The information obtained by means of this questionaire was then used to facilitate a more interpretive and detailed approach within nineteen schools in one small, clearly defined geographical area. The findings of this particular aspect of the research were published (*Schools Apart,* April 1977) and also form the bulk of Chapter 2 here. A brief comment on some of the conclusions is appropriate at this stage.

The most striking and consistent finding was the high level of mutual ignorance existing about schools attended by either major religious/ cultural group in Northern Ireland. Roman Catholics in general, and teachers in particular, know little about the activities within state (Protestant) schools. Often Protestant teachers profess to knowing nothing about 'what goes on' in Catholic schools. Such ignorance within one occupational group is naturally undesirable. In addition, the research suggested that out of this ignorance arises suspicion about the machinations of the 'alien' school system. Up until now, comment and debate upon schools in Northern Ireland has therefore tended to be uninformed and stereotyped.

This ignorance is in no way confined to the educational domain. Indeed it can be argued that the very existence of a general lack of knowledge between the two major cultural groups in Northern Ireland contributes significantly to the suspicion and intolerance which exists. Segregated schools, however, may contribute to and reinforce this separatism in society as a whole. It may well be that the cultural experiences undergone by children in such schools have an effect on their attitudes later in life.

It could also be that the problems associated with, or attributed to, segregated schooling may not be so much a result of the segregated structures themselves, but rather of the perceptions, attitudes and values of the individuals they serve. We simply don't know, and there is no information available for us to find out. Indeed, in this context, the *Schools Apart* report suggested that:

> perhaps a real understanding of school life in Northern Ireland can only be provided by means of an intensive study of a single school.

Previously, however, no one has had—or taken—the opportunity to study the cultures of such establishments in Northern Ireland at an in-depth level within the schools themselves. This prompted me to adopt a second mode of research which has become known as 'participant observation'. This entails becoming, as far as possible, an accepted member of the community or organisation under study, and is a strategy fraught with difficulty. It requires careful description, and any reader with a particular interest in research methodology is referred to the appendix.

Two primary schools were chosen for intensive study, one Roman Catholic, the other Protestant. I cannot claim that these schools are representative (in the statistical sense) of other primary schools in Northern Ireland. They are, however, both examples of such institutions and thus provide bases for generalisation. I say this only in so far as information gathered within, and insights emerging from, the schools will help to increase awareness and understanding of other schools which serve either community.

The two schools were chosen because they were among the nineteen schools selected for special study in the original *Schools Apart* research. They were both in the same geographical area – actually they were sited only 300 metres from each other – they had the same number of staff and pupils and, in addition, the backgrounds of the staff of each school were remarkably similar.

All of these similarities might seem to demonstrate a fair degree of comparability, but a serious problem remains. Social research differs significantly from scientific research in the way variables are treated in the research milieu. In the laboratory, for example, all variables can be controlled in an attempt to study one particular factor in isolation. This is not possible in real life. In this context, although the schools I have called St Judes and Rathlin seemed to have sufficient common features to justify comparison, they differed considerably in the social class backgrounds of their respective pupils. The principal of St Judes described his school as 'mainly working class' while Mr Long, in Rathlin, characterised his as being 'more middle class than most'.

It may be argued, therefore, that differences which emerged in practice between the two schools can be accounted for as much by social class composition as by religious or cultural factors. The researcher must be aware of these limitations when observing and commenting upon phenomena in such situations. This is essential if decisions are to be made about the relative influence of the many interrelated elements affecting behaviour in any social context. This decision-making process can cause problems because the objectivity of those making the choices and selection must be considered.

My credentials, therefore, must be stated unequivocally: I was 'born and bred' a Northern Irish Catholic, I attended a Catholic primary school and Catholic secondary school, and the social network in which I moved in my formative years was confined almost exclusively to my co-religionists. This inevitably resulted in my having a whole range of values and attitudes which are an intrinsic aspect of Catholicism in Ulster. It also means being inclined to perceive the social world in a particular, and perhaps narrow, way. Even if I were to try to 'slough off' these atavistic influences, they still lie so close to the surface that they are wont to appear on the most unexpected occasions.

It might be imagined that this background will inevitably result in bias in observation and description. This, however, is only the case if the observer is unaware of it. In the event, my awareness of the possibility of personal bias actually made it easier to understand the teachers in the schools and the influences which helped to shape their attitudes and values.

Nonetheless, the strategy of participant observation is not an easy one to adopt. It requires considerable self-discipline and a constant examination of one's preconceptions and assumptions. However, the year spent in full-time involvement with the everyday life of both schools yielded a richness of insight and information which I am convinced no other research method can produce.

The purpose of this book is two-fold. In the first place it attempts to describe and comment upon the day-to-day practices in two schools belonging to different cultures in Northern Ireland in an effort to alleviate the ignorance presently existing about and between them. Secondly, it studies the actual cultural experiences and practices within the schools in an effort to discover the extent to which the oft-stated claim that these experiences encourage devisiveness can be justified. In this sense it seeks to determine the extent to which the schools reflect, reinforce or counteract the cultural and social norms of the communities which they serve.

There can be no tolerance without comprehension and no comprehension without knowledge. Since schools in Northern Ireland epitomise the segregated nature of the state as a whole, it is vital that in-depth studies are carried out within them in order to gather and publish information about them. These may well contribute the bases, at least, for more mutual understanding.

1

The Origin and Growth
of Segregation

IN ORDER to examine the roles which schools play in Northern Ireland one has to be aware of the origin and growth of segregated schooling and also the social factors which have influenced this growth. It would be misguided to attempt such a cultural analysis of schools in Northern Ireland without taking into account the complex web of interrelating factors which form the overall culture of the major groups there. These include religion, history, tradition, politics and values. This chapter attempts to place present-day segregated schools in the context of both their historical development and modern perceptions and attitudes existing about them.

Historical Development

Historically, schooling in Ireland had been shaped more by clerics than by educationalists. Religious issues have been dominant in the passing or rejection of every education bill since 1800. Indeed, long before the nineteenth century, religion and education were inextricably meshed and the resulting evolution was typified more by tension than by tolerance.

In the sixteenth century, for example, Henry VIII instructed the Anglican clergy in Ireland to set up schools to promote both the English language and Protestantism among the Catholic masses. In fact, throughout the seventeenth century, successive repressive acts forbad Catholics to teach in Protestant schools, to keep their own schools, to employ tutors at home or to send their children abroad to be educated. Catholics were, however, encouraged to attend the Protestant establishments, but they steadfastly refused to do so.

Catholic children got their education by means of illegal classes which took place in the open country, with lookouts posted to warn of any approaching authorities. These became known, for obvious reasons, as 'hedge schools' and by the end of the eighteenth century, the bulk of Catholic education was being achieved in this way. Darby (1976) comments that 'the (very) Celto-Catholic culture which the Penal Laws were designed to subvert, continued to flourish illegally'. The hedge schools did in fact represent the first attempt by the Catholic population to have their own system of education, and it might be argued that the protracted and severe labour pains that were experienced then may well explain Catholic attitudes to later state intervention in the field of education and schooling in general.

However, while Darby (1976) may give the impression that the *raison d'être* of hedge schools was to preserve 'Celto-Catholic culture', this does not in fact seem to have been the case. Many, especially in the north of Ireland, were attended by Protestants. (Dr Henry Cooke, a famous orthodox Presbyterian, was one such case.) Also, neither religious teaching nor Irish culture seem to have figured highly on the curricula of hedge schools. In fact Dowling (1971) claims that they were instrumental in bringing about the decline of the Irish language in some areas by teaching all subjects in English. Several references have been made about the subjects taught in hedge schools. Gordon (1832) describes them as 'receptacles of rags and penury, in which a semi-barbarous peasantry acquired the rudiments of reading, writing, Irish history and high treason'. While some such schools were run by the local priest, the great majority were not, and reading, writing and arithmetic were the only subjects taught. Significantly, references to the teaching of religion in hedge schools are extremely rare.

This raises an interesting point with regard to the current debate about the integration of Protestant and Catholic schools in Northern Ireland. The fact that Catholicism and 'Celto-Catholic culture' flourished in Ireland during a period in which little or no religious instruction was given in schools would seem to weaken the present Roman Catholic segregationalist point of view that the school must exist as a means of reproducing the cultural and religious heritage. The claim that the Catholic school is essential for ensuring future generations of good Catholics also seems doubtful. It must be said, however, that hedge schools were never part of a mass educational system such as exists now, and so were not considered of the same importance by the Catholic hierarchy. Also, the overtly Catholic school may well have been conceived to counteract Protestant proselytising, whereas before the Catholic bishops were prepared to accept secular National schooling.

The year 1812 seems to represent a turning point in the approach to education in Ireland by the British government. In that year a commission of enquiry reported:

> We conceive it to be of essential importance in any new establishments for the education of the lower classes in Ireland, and we venture to express our unanimous opinion that no such plan, however wisely or unexceptionally contrived in other respects, can be carried into effectual execution in this country, unless it be explicitly avowed and clearly understood that no attempt shall be made to influence or disturb the peculiar religious tenets of any sect or description of Christians.

Just at this time Protestant groups and societies, who were both overtly and covertly proselytising bodies, abounded in Ireland. The Kildare Place Society, however, seemed most likely to reflect the intentions of the 1812 commissioners' report. It proposed 'to afford the same educational advantages to all classes of professing Christians, without interfering with the peculiar religious opinions of any'. The stipulation that the Bible should be read daily 'without note or comment', while causing some concern to the Catholic clergy, was neatly dealt with: they simply used the school Bible readings as the texts for the following Sunday's mass. Hence, while there was no 'note or comment' in school, there certainly was later! The mixed schools were therefore welcomed by the Irish bishops, and many Catholic parents sent their children to them. (They did fall from favour later when it was revealed that the Society was funding self-confessed proselytising bodies whose aims were to free Catholics from 'priestly domination' and 'the mummery of the mass house'!) The point of interest, however, is that the Catholic church in Ireland had accepted the principle of mixed schooling as long as there was no proselytising taking place within it.

A government awareness of this acceptance of mixed schooling by the bishops may well have facilitated the establishment, in 1831, of a National School System, the first such system in Europe. The basic tenet of the commission was to provide mixed education for children of different creeds and to avoid even the suspicion of proselytising.

Three points, however, caused problems: Bible readings, although obligatory, were to be excluded from the secular day, all clergy were to have free access to the schools and children were to be excluded from religious instruction given by a person from another faith.

Although the Catholic hierachy grudgingly accepted the system, the Protestant clergy reacted (sometimes violently) against it. They saw it as an attempt to eventually exclude the Bible altogether, and the Presbyterians especially were appalled by the possibility of Catholic clergy having access to 'their' schools. In addition, they claimed that Catholic children would only ever be subjected to heresy, i.e. there would be no chance of Protestant evangelisation.

In 1840, as a result of prolonged and bitter campaigning by the Protestant clergy, the government capitulated to their demands and amended all three 'offensive' articles to the clergy's satisfaction, and comparative calm reigned – in the Protestant camp at least. Not surprisingly, however, there seems to have been a direct relationship between the number of concessions granted to the Protestant churches by the commissioners and the growth of suspicion and concern among the Catholic bishops. They claimed that the original safeguards against proselytising were being eroded and they reacted predictably. In fact, only intervention by the Pope, Gregory XVI, obviated a mass withdrawal by Catholics from the National School System. Attitudes were hardening, however, and by the middle of the nineteenth century the more extreme Catholic clerics were insisting on 'a Catholic education, on Catholic principles with Catholic masters and the use of Catholic books' (Cullen, 1859).

Towards the end of the century, so many concessions had been granted by the commissioners to both sides (with regard to religious instruction) that all National schools had become *de facto* denominational institutions and remained so until the establishment of the state of Northern Ireland in 1921.

Magee (1971) sees this eventual denominationalism of schools in terms of each church getting what it wanted. He contends that the Protestant churches resented the National system mainly because it obstructed their work of evangelisation among Irish children of all faiths; the Catholic bishops only concerned themselves with the education of children of their own denomination. For whatever reason, however, it is important to note than even at this stage of history both

Catholics and Protestants had in reality their own denominational schools and each received *equal* financial assistance from the government.

In 1921, responsibility for education was removed from Dublin and transferred to the new Ministry of Education in Belfast. The first Minister of Education, Lord Londonderry, appointed a committee under the leadership of Robert Lynn to plan the reform of the Northern Ireland educational system. This committee reported back in September 1921. It was totally boycotted by the Catholic side, who were confident that the new state of Northern Ireland would never last.

The committee recommended that three classes of elementary schools be set up:

Class I: those built by local authorities or the ministry or those handed over to the ministry by the previous managers.

Class II: those schools with special management committees composed of four representatives of the former managers and two of the local government authorities.

Class III: those schools whose managers wished to remain entirely independant of the local government authorities.

The Class I schools were termed 'provided or transferred' schools and were to receive 100 per cent grants for both capital expenditure and maintenance. Class II ('maintained') were to receive about 82 per cent grant for capital expenditure and 50 per cent for maintenance, and Class III ('voluntary') schools were to receive only a grant for heating and cleaning.

Lynn also recommended that religious instruction should be given and that teachers should be required to teach it. This religion should be taught within school hours. These recommendations placed Lord Londonderry in a difficult position. Akenson (1973) succinctly explains why: Northern Ireland's populace refused to accept secular education, hence moral education was compulsory in all schools; to the Ulster Protestant clergy, moral education necessarily included Bible instruction, but to require Bible instruction, while prohibiting the commentary of the church fathers, was to enforce the teaching of Protestantism, since the Catholic church held that scriptures had to be interpreted in the light of the church's traditions. Hence, to require

Bible instruction during school hours was to implicitly establish and endow the Protestant faith, but such endorsement was prohibited by the government of Ireland Act, 1920.

Londonderry's subsequent Education Act of 1923 substantially amended Lynn's recommendations with regard to religious instruction. It stated that religious instruction was to be excluded from the secular day and that teachers could not be compelled to teach it. He argued that this was the only course open to him since the 1920 act forbade the government of Northern Ireland to 'make a law so as either directly or indirectly to establish or endow any religion'. The three main Protestant churches in Northern Ireland were outraged by Londonderry's 1923 Act. Their rancour was three-pronged and was reflected in their insistence that government authorities should provide for Bible instruction, teachers should teach it, and teachers should not, as had been suggested in the act, be appointed at local government level but rather by a central committee. Their concern was that in areas with a Catholic majority in local government, Catholic teachers might be appointed to Class I schools. A clarion call to Protestants at the time was, 'The door is thrown open for a Bolshevist or an atheist or a Roman Catholic to become a teacher in a Protestant *(sic)* school'. The call seems to have been clear – 'Protestant teachers for Protestant schools' – and by 1925 only ten out of 2,000 operating elementary schools had transferred to state control.

The pressure from the Protestant clergy and the Orange Order became so intense that the Prime Minister, Sir James Craig, rushed through an amendment in March 1925 which seemed to make three main concessions to the Protestant clergy: in Class I schools teachers should teach religious instruction; the provision banning local authorities from providing religious instruction was deleted; and school management committees could advise local authorities on the appointment of teachers.

Comparative peace reigned for about two years. It was then learned that some County Borough education committees were not complying with the 1925 Amendment Act in 'requiring' teachers to teach religious instruction in Class I schools. Once again the Protestant clergy gave vent to their ill feelings. It was also about this time that the Catholic hierarchy entered the fray. It might be argued that had they done so sooner they might have found themselves less disadvantaged, at least financially, than they were. Akenson (1973) goes further, saying, 'The fact that Roman Catholics were not represented on the Lynn committee (1921) was the single most important determinant (in the shaping of) the educational system of Northern Ireland'. In any case their interest now was mainly financial, and they cried out for 75 per cent grants for Class III (i.e. voluntary) schools. The Protestant clergy, on the other hand, were insisting on increased guarantees about the selection and subsequent behaviour of teachers. The 1930 Education Act would seem to have appeased both groups to a greater or lesser degree.

1. County Borough education committees and Class I school management committees were required to appoint to their boards a certain percentage (25 per cent to the former and at least 50 per cent to the latter) from those who had transferred their schools. This meant in effect that the Protestant clergy for the first time now had an official voice at both local government and school management level.
2. Teachers in Class I schools were required by law to teach religious instruction.
3. Class III schools were to receive 50 per cent capital expenditure grants and 50 per cent towards maintenance.

Fifteen years of unprecedented serenity followed. By 1937, 50 per cent of non-Catholic elementary schools had transferred authority to the ministry.

The next event of major importance in shaping schooling in Northern Ireland was the government white paper of 1944. There were six main issues enunciated.

1. 'Voluntary' Class III schools were to receive grants of 65 per cent for capital expenditure and 65 per cent for maintenance (50 per cent and 50 per cent previously).
2. 'Maintained' Class II schools should receive 65 per cent capital expenditure and 100 per cent maintenance grants.
3. Children were to leave primary school at eleven years and proceed to secondary school until the age of fifteen years.
4. 'Provided or transferred' Class I schools were to become known as 'county' schools.
5 A conscience clause for teachers in county schools was introduced whereby no action could be taken against them if they refused to

teach religious instruction.

6. Religious instruction was to be excluded from the secular day in county schools.

Once more objections were raised by the churches, with the Protestant attack being much more vehement. They opposed grants to voluntary schools on the grounds that they represented an endowment of Roman Catholicism. The conscience clause for teachers also gave cause for concern since it was thought that teachers willing to teach religious instruction would be 'difficult to find'. The government however did not yield.

On the Catholic side it was argued that the raising of the school leaving age to fifteen years put added financial strain on managers. Sutherland (1973) records that there was not enough fiscal incentive offered to tempt voluntary schools to adopt the 'four and two' (Class II) system of management. Such committees also seem to have been seen by a sizeable minority of Catholics as representing the thin end of a governmental wedge.

It transpired that for almost the first time clerical pressure was resisted and the white paper, almost unchanged, became law in 1947. This act has shaped Northern Irish schools into basically what they are today. After the act almost all Protestant elementary schools transferred to become county (latterly known as 'state' or 'controlled') primary schools.

Catholic primary schools remained 'voluntarily' aloof until 1968 when an amendment act produced increased incentives for them to allow one third of their management committees to consist of government representatives (i.e. become 'four and two', or 'maintained'). Grants of 80 per cent towards capital expenditure were offered together with a 100 per cent grant for maintenance. The less suspicious Catholic managers acquiesced quite soon after this government amendment, and by the late 1970s almost all Catholic primary schools had become 'maintained'.

Today, Catholic children generally attend 'maintained' schools and Protestant children attend 'controlled/state' schools. However, teachers in the controlled sector often object to their schools being described as Protestant. They claim that they are open to all, and are thus non-denominational. This may well be so in theory, but enough evidence exists to demonstrate that controlled schools are *de facto* Protestant institutions, in composition at least – a point which I will discuss in more detail later. Of more concern here is the argument that state schools reflect the cultural aspirations of Protestant children as do Catholic schools those of Catholic children. I will return to this assertion in subsequent chapters.

Returning to the religious composition of schools in Northern Ireland, I should say at the outset that primary schools especially are almost totally polarised on religious lines. Chapter 2 provides quantitative evidence to support this, but a brief résumé will help here.

The data indicate that only 0.3 per cent of Roman Catholic teachers are employed in state primary schools. They also suggest that over 97 per cent of state primary schools have less than 5 per cent Catholic enrolment and over 98 per cent of Catholic schools have less than 5 per cent Protestant pupils. It is also worth noting that everyone interviewed during this research knew exactly what was meant by the 'Protestant' and 'Catholic' school. (That is, 'state' and 'maintained'.)

Numerically, therefore, they seem to be Protestant and Catholic establishments which are perceived as such by the local populace. Historically, it could be argued that one of the most consistent aspects in the development of Northern Irish primary schooling has been the sustained pressure from Protestant groups to obtain guarantees about religious considerations before, and after, the transfer of their schools to state control.

In 1923 the Protestant churches sought guarantees that local authorities would provide religious instruction in 'their' schools and that the teachers would be required to teach it. The former demand was achieved in 1925, and the latter in 1930.

The 1930 Education Act ensured Bible instruction within state schools. The Protestant clergy also negotiated at least 50 per cent representation on the management committees of state primary schools. The object of the act was seen as safeguarding the Protestant religion in state schools and at the same time retaining an un-denominational mien. After the passing of the act the Protestant churches expressed open satisfaction that 'the Protestant character of the state is (now) reflected in state schools'. (Campbell, 1964)

In fact throughout the history of Northern Irish primary schooling it is made clear, by inference at least, that state schools are considered to be Protestant establishments.

In the 1970's too there are examples of the statutory bodies (Department of Education and Education and Library Boards) recognising state schools as being *de facto* Protestant establishments. When a new controlled school – a state school entirely financed by public funds – is being built, representatives of the Protestant churches are approached to sit on its management committee. The Roman Catholic clergy are not. That Protestant teachers are considered more suitably employed in state schools is exemplified by the fact that every month a list of teaching post vacancies existing in state schools is circularised by the department to all state schools. The list is not sent to Catholic/maintained schools. (Murray, 1983)

The legal position with regard to bus fares is that financial help may be given if a child lives more than two miles from a *suitable* school. In practice this means that if there is a Catholic school within two miles of a Protestant child he may still receive financial help – it seems that only the state school is deemed *suitable* for the Protestant child.

It seems that enough evidence exists to justify describing state schools as Protestant, which is what I have done throughout this book.

Maintained schools are overtly and self-avowedly Catholic. The Roman Catholic Church regards the school as almost a *sine qua non* of church life. For example Archbishop Winning (1976) has described education as the 'essential expression of Christ's message'. He also claims that Catholic education unashamedly aims at locating the message of Christ, proclaimed by the Church, at the very heart of the syllabus, curriculum and life of the school community. There is also a long-standing church law making attendance at Catholic schools a matter of obligation in conscience. (This was graphically demonstrated to the staff in Rathlin when the local Catholic priest refused to give the sacraments to the few Catholic children who were attending their state school.)

There also seems to be a defensiveness implicit in the Roman Catholic view of schooling. Bishop Philbin (1975), in a statement which must have a profound effect on any attempt to integrate schools in Northern Ireland, claimed that:

There is no greater injury that can be done to Catholicism than interference with the character and identity of our schools.

This aspect of identity is continually emphasised:

The liturgy of the day should bring out the interdependence of home, school and church in the Christian formation of the young . . . . Children should be asked to wear school uniform to add to the visual effect.

I will deal with the whole question of identity more fully in Chapter 4. It is worth noting, however, that the children at St Jude's, in common with every other Catholic primary school in the area, wore green uniform. One might speculate that not only did this identity the schools as Catholic institutions (as Bishop Philbin requests), but also that the general preference for the colour green might well cause them to be perceived by Protestant commentators as fostering a particular political ideology.

In fact, very strong emphasis is placed by the Catholic hierarchy on this trinity of church, school and home. Cardinal Conway (1971) writes:

The Faith is given in Baptism but is fostered in life by the whole Christian community—family, school and church . . . schools co-operate with the family to foster, deepen, intensify and reinforce the faith initiated in the home . . . . Teachers never replace parents, together they make a formidable team, apart they leave gaps.

Cardinal O'Fiaich (1979) claims that the atmosphere of the schools is in tune with the atmosphere of the Catholic home. This concept of education is not only to be aspired towards – it must also be fought for as a right. The home is constantly exhorted to support the Catholic school, both ideologically and financially. The Sacred Congregation for Catholic Education (1977) insists that it is the duty of parents to support their schools, even at great personal cost. In fact, Catholic schools in Ireland have had to struggle to construct and maintain their own schools from penal times. The gradual process of emancipation since then has not yet resulted in equality of principle becoming equality in fact.

There are therefore both historic and economic reasons, apart from their religious *raison d'être,* for Catholic schools to be considered by both religious groups as different from state schools. It is a combination of such factors which has resulted in, on the one hand, a fierce commitment to their perpetuation and, on the other, a suspicion of what goes on within them.

It is rather more difficult to obtain and present what might be termed 'the Protestant view' of schooling in Northern Ireland. There are several reasons for this. In the first place the existence of so many different churches in the province (fifty-one named in the 1971 census), which can all loosely be described as Protestant, precludes the possibility of one consensual view.

Secondly, as Eric Gallagher (1977) claims:

> As long as Catholicism has insisted and still insists on its special role in education, so long the rest are absolved any requirement to articulate their position radically.

There is an additional factor. In 1929 the educational committees of the main Protestant churches expressed the demand that:

> The proposed legislation (for state schools) should be calculated to continue the interests of the (Protestant) churches in education and to foster an atmosphere in the schools friendly to the churches

and subsequently that the Education Act (1930) 'adequately reflected the Protestant nature of the state'. In fact, this act had the paradoxical effect of limiting the power of Protestant commentators to define the Protestant nature of state schools in any specific or exclusive manner. To do so would be tantamount to admitting that state schools are in fact Protestant establishments which officially and legally they are not.

All these factors may explain the comparative dearth of comment from the Protestant churches on education in Northern Ireland throughout the last forty years. The views that have been expressed have tended to be directed specifically towards the debate on segregated education or to emphasise the non-Roman Catholic (as distinct from Protestant) essence of state schools. In fact it can be argued that the Protestant approach to education has consistently been reactive in nature, i.e. the question was not so much that state schools should be specifically, or denominationally, Protestant but rather to ensure that no Catholic influence be tolerated. Much of the historic flavour of this rationale has already been presented; however, contemporary evidence also exists.

It should be remembered that state schools are officially open to all and thus non-denominational. It should also be emphasised that these schools are built and maintained entirely from public funds which are gathered through the taxation of Protestant and Catholic citizens alike. However, an event in 1981 demonstrates the Protestant expectation and the Catholic acceptance that state schools are in fact Protestant institutions.

In August of that year it became known that one of the Education and Library Boards had appointed two Catholic members to the management committee of a state school. Immediately a petition was prepared by Protestant parents, clergy and members of management committees of other state schools. This petition was submitted to the minister responsible for education, Lord Elton, demanding that the board should appoint only non-Catholic representatives to the management committees of state schools because 'in the vast majority of cases, pupils at state schools are Protestant'. The two Roman Catholic members subsequently resigned.

While much anecdotal evidence of this kind abounds in Northern Ireland, it is extremely difficult to find definitive accounts of the Protestant position. Gallagher's (1977) work provides a significant and salutary exception. His brief was to research the existing rationales of education in Northern Ireland and his findings provide the best, if not the only, exposition of these. It seems appropriate to reproduce his summary here.

1. 'We must not leave the education of our children in the hands of others.' That dictum was enunciated about one hundred years ago. Whether the others were Roman Catholics, other Protestants or agnostics one hundred years ago is not quite clear. Today the issue is less open to argument. The fact of the matter is beyond dispute in spite of all that a century of secularisation and increasing materialism has done to us. The vast majority of parents want their children educated – and I use the phrase without intending any disparagement – by 'their own sort'.

2. 'Matters of controversy or suggestions of sedition should be eliminated from text-books.' Here we touch on one of the most sensitive areas and on convictions which though they may not often be articulated are none the less deeply felt. There you have a phrase used for the first time not yesterday or last year but during World

War 1. That phrase encapsulates all the real fears and suspicions of a Gaelic Catholic culture. One of the fears that the vast majority of Protestant parents have hitherto had and indeed still have, is that to involve their children in integrated education would be in some way to expose them to a Gaelic Catholic culture with which they wish to have nothing to do and which in some way could—indeed would—result in a loss of their Britishness.

3. Requirements with regard to the religious instruction of children. The early controversies surrounding this issue in the Northern Parliament sprang from convictions that are by no means dead. There is a fear that integrated education could lead either to the disappearance altogether of biblically based religious instruction or, what might be considered worse, the development of a watered down form of bible instruction or a Catholic coloured one. Many Protestant parents may not be distinguished for assiduous church attendance or religious practice. No matter, they know what they want and don't want for their children. Bible-based religious instruction is a must, and they believe that they are more likely to get it in a segregated school (of the Protestant kind, of course) than in a Catholic one.

4. 'The need to foster in the schools an atmosphere friendly to the Churches.' This is hard to describe or define exactly but it has to do with ethos, tradition and values. Religion is part and parcel of Irish tradition – north and south. Just as Catholicism has laid great stress on the need to move its schools with the traditions, influences and ethos on which the Catholic church has laid great stress, so too, rightly or wrongly, the Protestant churches and Protestant parents have felt that a segregated system (provided satisfactory arrangements can be reached with the state regarding management, and taking into account Roman Catholic non-participation in state schools) is more likely than an integrated one to produce that ethos, safeguard the values and develop the traditions.

5. Those who lived or agonised during the bitter debate that finally led to the provision of a 'conscience clause' enabling teachers to opt out of religious instruction will recognise another rationale. It was the insistence not only on a biblically-based curriculum for religious instruction, but the conviction that that instruction could best be given by those who were then themselves convinced about it and

about teaching it. Again, rightly or wrongly, many who fought this battle did so not only to release honest teachers from a task for which they had no conviction, but also to secure teachers who had. And they believed that the kind of teachers they wanted for the task were more likely to be found in a segregated school.

6. Again and again in recent years reference has been made to parental choice. It is considered all important in the forthcoming re-organisation of secondary education to make maximum possible provision for the exercise of such choice. Parental choice is recognised as a human right. Segregated education is the order of the day because that is the way that parents want it. There is no evidence that they want it any other way. There is much to suggest that any attempt to enforce a change would provoke intense and widespread opposition.

7. Mixed marriages: the Church of Ireland may have been the only one to refer to mixed marriages in its response to the report on 'Violence in Ireland', but it is not the only one to feel deeply about the matter. Mixed marriages are a burning issue. I make no comment on the reasons for the feeling they engender. They are there and as long as they are there and the reasons for them remain, so long will most parents, Protestants and Catholic, be less than enthusiastic about any educational or cultural institution that makes too much integrated provision for their young people. Segregated schools are a safer bet than integrated ones.

Implicit in almost all of these points is the fact that religion is 'part and parcel' of tradition and indeed political identity in Northern Ireland. Indeed it may well be for this reason that any defence of the Protestant nature of state schools has been articulated as often by politicians as by clergy or educators. For example, Dr Hugh Morrison, a Member of Parliament for Queen's University, referring to the possibility of regional education committees being established in 1923 and their possible influence on schools, claimed that:

> In some areas where Catholics were in the majority they would have the power to appoint teachers to Protestant *(sic)* schools. . . . This is a situation that the Protestant Church will not submit to.

Also the passing of the 1930 Education Act for Northern Ireland was generally acclaimed as the conception of a state system of education which would 'maintain the Protestant character of the state'. Again, a Northern Ireland Member of Parliament, Joseph Morgan, claimed in a government debate in November 1946 that:

It is not too much to ask that a Protestant Government elected by a Protestant people, should maintain that we should have Protestant teachers for Protestant children.

Tony Spencer (1974), a member of the Belfast Education and Library Board claimed that:

The state is building denominational schools, since their Boards of Management were comprised of at least one half by direct representation of the Protestant Churches.

(And no representatives of the Catholic Church.)

In a cultural analysis of primary schools in Northern Ireland it is essential to document and emphasise the religious aspect of both systems of schooling in order to demonstrate that they serve two religious systems; one Roman Catholic and the other Protestant. It is vital that this fact be established since, in Northern Ireland, one's religion is the single greatest determinant of the culture to which one belongs. In fact Bishop Daly (1980) sees the fundamental task of schooling as 'a sythesis of culture and faith'. It can be claimed that religious, cultural and national identity here are coincident. It is not claimed, however, that the school is the sole agent for maintaining this immutable trinity but rather that it is one important contributor to such a reality.

Other commentators have tended to over-emphasise this role of the school. Spencer (1974), for example, argues that 'religious identities, fostered in the two church school systems form the basis for national identity'. This statement, in neglecting the influence of home and peers, seems to elevate the importance of the schools as a creator of attitudes and values to an unrealistic level.

However, the focus of this book is the school, and from observation within schools it seems clear that there is indeed emphasis on separate and different cultures. In St Jude's a nationalist, and to a lesser extent, Gaelic culture was fostered. There was evidence of what Farren (1976) has referred to as 'attempts to idealise the indigenous cultures to provide an attractive alternative to that propagated by the colonial (i.e. Protestant) power. In Rathlin the atmosphere was much more clearly British. Almost by definition, the cultural roots of members of a colonial power must lie elsewhere. In the case of Rathlin they seemed to emanate more from Scotland and England than Ireland.

This necessitates not only a cultural analysis of the school but also a political one, since again the two are almost synonymous. In fact religion may be seen to be of secondary importance to political affilitation, with the former being merely a convenient or overt indication of the latter. An advertisement which appeared in the *Belfast Telegraph* demonstrates the point:

Wanted – reliable cook, general – Protestant. (Christian preferred.)

Most studies in Northern Ireland of segregated schooling have, unfortunately, failed to recognise this subtle connection. Analogies have, therefore, been drawn with segregated schools in the rest of the world and in mainland Britain. Such analogies cannot and should not be used.

McCloskey (1962) commenting on American schools has demonstrated that parochial school Catholics were subsequently as involved in community affairs as anyone else in the community. However, the situation in America is not identical with Northern Ireland. There is not an institutional alienation simply because one is a Catholic.

Also in Britain, pupils can attend a Jesuit college or Church of England school and subsequently vote Liberal, Labour or Conservative. They may also all still share a common cultural heritage. In America, black children can attend all-black schools and still vote either Republican or Democrat. In Northern Ireland, however, it would be almost inconceivable for a Catholic child who attended a maintained school to subsequently vote Unionist or, indeed, a Protestant who has attended a state school to cast his vote for a Republican. In other words, the broad political affiliation of any individual in Northern Ireland is a function of his religion and consequently of the school which he attended.

It would seem, therefore, that the constellation of political, cultural and religious influences experienced by children in their separate schools is worthy of very serious consideration.

2

Schools Apart:
The Extent of Segregation

IT HAS been claimed in the previous chapter that the broad cultural and political affiliations of individuals in Northern Ireland are functions of their religion and hence of the schools which they attended. Obviously this claim is premised on the conviction that schools in the province are polarised on religious grounds. It also implies that the experiences of Protestant and Catholic children are significantly different within their segregated schools. However, little research evidence exists which either quantifies the degree of polarisation or illuminates the disparate experiences of children in these schools.

This chapter attempts to redress the prevailing lack of knowledge about educational segregation by presenting research data on the subject which hitherto has been available only to a very small academic audience. The inclusion of such data is also deemed essential to provide a general context for the more specific and interpretative observations and analyses which comprise the bulk of subsequent chapters.

In 1964 official statistics ceased to include information on the denominational distribution of school pupils. In the following years, no reliable data were produced on the subject. The resulting lack of knowledge about segregated schools has served to make debate on the subject both ill-formed and sterile. It also motivated a group of researchers (myself included), based at the new University of Ulster, to attempt to quantify the degree of separation and present a profile of educational practice in segregated schools. This report *(Schools Apart)* was published in 1977.

A questionnaire, covering many aspects of school life, was issued to a representative sample of schools in Northern Ireland (32 grammar, 68 secondary and 150 primary) and 159 schools responded. The analysis of the data is presented here under five main categories: pupils and teachers; management and organisation; school and community; religious practices; curricular and extra-curricular activities.

31

The returns are also organised under what may appear to be the rather abritrary headings of 'Catholic' and 'Protestant' schools. While such an approach can be argued to present a realistic portrayal of segregated schools in Northern Ireland, the main reason for its use here is to facilitate ease of reading and comprehension.

Pupils and Teachers

Table 2:1
ROMAN CATHOLIC PUPILS IN NORTHERN IRISH SCHOOLS (PER CENT)

% Roman Catholic pupils	Protestant Schools			Catholic Schools		
	Gr.	Sec.	Prim.	Gr.	Sec.	Prim.
0	18.2	63.6	67.2	—	—	—
less than 1	9.1	—	5.2	—	—	—
1–5	45.4	22.7	19.0	—	—	—
6–9	—	—	—	—	—	—
10–19	9.1	9.1	3.4	—	—	—
20–29	—	—	—	—	—	—
30–39	—	—	—	—	—	—
40–49	—	—	—	—	—	—
50–59	—	—	—	—	—	—
60–69	—	—	—	—	—	—
70–79	—	—	—	—	—	—
80–89	—	—	—	—	—	—
90–94	—	—	—	—	—	—
95–99	—	—	—	20	22.7	7.3
100	—	—	—	80	77.3	90.3
No response	18.2	4.6	5.2	0	0	2.4
TOTAL	100	100	100	100	100	100

The returns support the view that Protestant and Roman Catholic school-children in Northern Ireland attend schools where their co-religionists predominate. None of the 67 Roman Catholic schools which responded to the question had less than a 95 per cent Roman Catholic school population and 58 of them (86.6 per cent) were attended exclusively by Roman Catholic pupils. Of the 84 Protestant schools which responded only 5 (5.9 per cent) had a Roman Catholic population of more than 5 per cent and 55 schools (65.5 per cent) had no Roman Catholic pupils at all.

Table 2:2

ROMAN CATHOLIC TEACHERS IN PROTESTANT SCHOOLS (PER CENT)

Type of School	Number of Schools responding	Total number of teachers	Mean % Roman Catholic teachers
Grammar	10	341	1.33
Secondary	22	756	2.20
Primary	58	466	0.30*

(* totally accounted for by 2 schools)

Table 2:3

PROTESTANT TEACHERS IN ROMAN CATHOLIC SCHOOLS (PER CENT)

Type of School	Number of Schools responding	Total number of teachers	Mean % Protestant teachers
Grammar	3	139	0.60
Secondary	22	765	1.60
Primary	41	283	0.50*

(* totally accounted for by 1 school)

The degree of polarisation of Protestant and Catholic schools is well reflected in the number of teachers employed in schools of different religious affiliation to their own. The percentages cited in the tables, when translated into actual numbers of teachers, confirm this:

1. Of the 1,521 secondary teachers considered in the survey only 29 were employed in schools where the predominant religious affiliation was different to their own.
2. Of 480 grammar school teachers studied, only 9 were thus employed.
3. Of 750 primary school teachers in the survey, only 3 were employed in schools of different religion. In fact only 3 primary schools (out of 99) employed any teachers from the other category.

Questions were also asked about the educational backgrounds of teachers. As was anticipated, the percentage of graduate teachers in grammar schools was high—84.7 per cent in Catholic and 100 per cent in Protestant, although only two Protestant schools responded to the question. At secondary school level 45.5 per cent of teachers in Protestant schools were graduates, compared to 39 per cent in Catholic schools. Although the number of graduates in primary schools was naturally smaller, the difference in percentages was more marked – 15 per cent of all teachers in Protestant schools, compared to 7.4 per cent in Catholic schools.

Table 2:4

TEACHERS TRAINED IN BRITAIN (PER CENT)

School Type	Protestant	Catholic
Grammar	10.0	4.8
Secondary	5.2	19.6
Primary	5.4	33.2

Table 2:4 displays interesting differences in the academic histories of teachers employed in Protestant and Catholic schools. At secondary and primary level there are more teachers from the Catholic schools trained in Britain than Protestant. Since only two Catholic grammar schools responded to this question, it is inadvisable to draw conclusions at this level. A truly remarkable figure of 33.2 per cent of Catholic primary teachers had at least some of their training there. (When this point was put later to Catholic teachers they showed little surprise. It was explained by the contention that Roman Catholics until recently regarded teaching as a first-choice occupation with better promotion possibilities than the civil service or local government. As a result, competition for places in the Catholic colleges of education was believed to be intense and many Catholics went further afield for their training than their Protestant counterparts.)

Management and Organisation

Management Bodies

In general Catholic schools are managed by smaller committees at both secondary and primary levels. All responding grammar schools in both categories had more than six members on their management boards. The continued existence of a small number of schools managed by a single individual (one Protestant and two Catholic) is a reminder of the time when single-manager schools were more common than any other form of management structure.

Table 2:5

NUMBER OF MEMBERS ON MANAGEMENT BODY

Number of members	Protestant Gr.	Sec.	Prim.	Catholic Gr.	Sec.	Prim.
One	—	—	1.7	—	—	4.9
6 or less	—	—	6.9	—	36.4	56.1
More than 6	90.9	100	89.7	100	63.6	36.6
No response	9.1	—	1.7	—	—	2.4
TOTAL	100	100	100	100	100	100

The interests represented on management committees differ, to some degree, between different types of schools. All responding grammer schools, for example, have representation from the Department of Education, which only applied to four other schools – all Protestant – in the entire sample. There are greater similarities in the number of schools with teachers and parents on their management committees.

Table 2:6

SCHOOLS WITH TEACHERS ON MANAGEMENT COMMITTEES (PER CENT)

Protestant Gr.	Sec.	Prim.	Catholic Gr.	Sec.	Prim.
18.2	0	19	20	4.5	4.8

While teacher representation is very unusual in secondary schools, both Protestant and Catholic grammar schools have similar levels. Catholic primary schools have a smaller teacher representation on management bodies than their Protestant counterparts. This might be explained, to some extent, by the fact that management bodies tend to be smaller in Catholic primary schools.

Table 2:7

SCHOOLS WITH PARENTS ON MANAGEMENT COMMITTEE
(PER CENT)

Number of Parents	Protestant			Catholic		
	Gr.	Sec.	Prim.	Gr.	Sec.	Prim.
None	18.2	—	6.9	20	72.7	48.8
One	9.1	—	—	20	22.7	9.8
Two or more	63.7	95.5	89.61	45	4.6	36.6
No response	9.0	4.5	3.5	15	—	4.8
TOTAL	100	100	100	100	100	100

Formal representation of parents on management bodies is much more common in Protestant schools than Catholic. In fact the percentages of Catholic secondary and primary schools without any parental representation are high.

It is also notable that within Catholic schools parental representation is much more extensively practised at primary than at secondary level, perhaps suggesting greater parental interest at this level. It may be that the Catholic clergy see themselves as being representatives of the parents, thus making formal representation of the latter superfluous. It is relevant to point out that the Education and Library Board Order (1972) requires Protestant schools to have parental representation on their management committees, and that it has nothing to say about parental representation in Catholic schools.

Management committees of Protestant schools meet rather more often than those of Catholic schools. Taken with the involvement of the principal in the management structure (Table 2:8 following) the impression given is of more continuous involvement by the management body, on the formal level, in Protestant schools.

Table 2:8

FREQUENCY OF MANAGEMENT COMMITTEE MEETINGS

Frequency	Protestant			Catholic		
	Gr.	Sec.	Prim.	Gr.	Sec.	Prim.
Once	—	—	12.1	—	—	2.4
1–3 times	9.1	50	63.8	100	77.3	75.6
More than 3 times	81.8	50	20.7	—	22.7	9.8
No response	9.1	—	3.4	—	—	12.2
TOTAL	100	100	100	100	100	100

There is a general indication that the principal has more formal status and more access to management committees in Protestant schools than in Catholic. Particularly notable, for example, is the very high percentage (34.1 per cent) of Catholic primary school principals who only attend management committee meetings when invited. In the second stage of the study, principals from both catergories expressed dissatisfaction with the system.

Table 2:9
PRIMARY SCHOOL PRINCIPALS – TIME ALLOCATION

Activity	Principals giving 'none' response (per cent)	
	Protestant	Catholic
Contact with parents	20.7	22.0
Contact with teachers	17.2	17.1
General administration	3.4	12.2
Informal contact with pupils	34.5	41.5
Teaching	7.3	6.9

Principals were asked about the distribution of their own working activities. Apart from grammar schools, the majority of principals do some teaching, and at primary level it constitutes more than half their working time for the majority of principals. One marked difference between Protestant and Catholic schools, however, is the fact that in secondary schools, 77.3 per cent of Protestant principals teach for at least part of their time, while this applies to only 54.5 per cent of Catholic principals.

Among primary school principals, a surprisingly large percentage indicated that they did not involve themselves in some activities where one might have expected time would be spent (see Table 2:9).

Discipline

Table 2:10
FORMS OF DISCIPLINE PRACTISED IN SCHOOLS (PER CENT)

Form of Discipline	Protestant			Catholic		
	Gr.	Sec	Prim.	Gr.	Sec.	Prim.
A Corporal punishment	—	81.8	41.4	40.0	81.8	48.8
B Suspension	36.4	40.9	—	60.0	63.6	4.9
C Expulsion	36.4	—	1.7	40.0	18.2	4.9
D Detention	63.6	72.7	34.5	80.0	63.6	12.2
E Extra work	54.5	81.8	55.2	80.0	59.1	26.8
F Deprivation of privileges	45.5	86.4	63.8	40.0	77.3	65.9

The high incidence of corporal punishment in secondary and primary schools in both categories is notable, and particularly its use in more than four out of every five secondary schools.

If A and B are considered as 'high level' controls, and D, E and F as 'low level' controls, then there is a suggestion that Catholic schools are more punishment-oriented than Protestant. It should be remembered that controlled schools have no power to expel pupils.

Table 2:11

MAINTENANCE OF DISCIPLINE BY PUPILS (PER CENT)

Form of discipline	Protestant			Catholic		
	Gr.	Sec.	Prim.	Gr.	Sec.	Prim.
Corporal punishment	—	—	—	—	—	—
Detention	27.3	13.6	—	20	—	2.4
Extra work	27.3	9.1	1.7	—	4.5	—
Report (to teachers)	72.7	63.6	27.6	80	68.2	53.7
Others	18.2	12.7	13.8	—	—	14.6

Protestant schools appear to place more reliance upon the participation of pupils in the maintenance of discipline. This may well be related to their use of what have already been described as 'low level' controls, which may lend themselves more to pupil involvement.

It is also worth noting that, while many measures of educational practice in Northern Irish schools present a general picture of 'traditional' rather than 'liberal' schools, not a single school in the sample permitted pupils to apply corporal punishment to other pupils.

School and Community

It was hypothesised that, if there were any significant differences between the two catergories of schools, they would be particularly manifest in the nature of their relationships with the community. This was examined in some detail during subsequent interviews, but a number of questions were also included in the questionnaire.

Table 2:12

PRESENCE OF PARENTS' OR PARENT-TEACHER ASSOCIATION
IN SCHOOL (PER CENT)

Association	Protestant			Catholic		
	Gr.	Sec.	Prim.	Gr.	Sec.	Prim.
Parents Association or PTAs	63.6	50.0	32.7	40	18.2	4.8
No Parents' Association or PTA	27.3	50.0	65.6	60	81.8	90.4
No response	9.1	—	1.7	—	—	4.8
TOTAL	100	100	100	100	100	100

Parents' and parent-teacher associations are not popular in Northern Ireland. Only 45 of the 159 sample schools (28.5 per cent) have such associations, rather more in grammar than secondary schools. In primary schools they are quite rare, only operating in 21.2 per cent of schools.

Parents' or parent-teacher associations are more common in Protestant than in Catholic schools at every level. None of the Catholic schools are affiliated to the Northern Ireland Parents' Association, while 18.9 per cent of Protestant schools are affiliated. All 45 of the associations meet at least twice a year, 33 of them (73.3 per cent) more than three times each year. The main activities carried out by parents' or parent-teacher associations are cultural or educational activities, social activities and fund-raising. A surprisingly small proportion, especially in Protestant schools, advise pupils on careers.

The incidence of ex-pupils' associations in schools is more closely related to the type of school than to its denominational mix. Of the 92 primary schools responding to the question, 91 (98.9 per cent) have no ex-pupils' association; nor have 39 of the 44 responding secondary schools (88.6 per cent). On the other hand, all 15 of the responding grammar schools have one.

Of the 21 schools with ex-pupils' associations the most common activities are social, followed by sports, cultural/educational activities and fund raising. Cultural or educational activities are markedly more common in Catholic schools' ex-pupils associations than in those of Protestant schools; 71.4 per cent of their associations are involved in such activities, compared to only 14.3 per cent of Protestant schools.

Perhaps a more significant measure of a school's relationship with its neighbourhood than the presence of either parents' or ex-pupils' associations is its involvement in community projects.

Table 2:13

SCHOOLS WITH PUPILS INVOLVED IN SCHOOL-BASED
COMMUNITY PROJECTS (PER CENT)

Project type	Protestant	Catholic
Study projects	8.8	11.8
Working with elderly	25.3	22.0
Working with children	20.9	14.7
Working with young people	4.4	2.9
Working with sick	12.1	10.3
Other activities	7.7	7.4
No responses	48.3	51.5

The question about the involvement of pupils in school-based community projects, curricular and extra-curricular, met with the largest number of non-responses in the entire questionaire, with 79 schools (49.7 per cent) not answering the question. Consequently the positive responses should be treated with caution.

Of the 151 schools responding to the question about the availability of school premises to the public, 55 (36.4 per cent) were not available to the public outside school hours. There is little difference in the practices of Protestant and Catholic schools, except at primary school level. There, 66.7 per cent of Catholic schools were not available, compared to 40.7 per cent of Protestant schools. Schools were more available in the evenings (70.2 per cent of all schools) than at weekends (17.9 per cent of all schools). There was little difference in the activities carried out by the public in Protestant and Catholic schools.

Whatever the reasons for more than one-third of all schools not being available to the public, the violence of recent years is not a major factor. Only 4 schools in the survey (2.5 per cent) considered that the use of the school by the public had been abandoned as a result of the violence, and only 25 (15.7 per cent) that it had been curtailed.

Religious Practices

A total of five questions concentrated on the formal religious activities and teaching in the schools, and, in general, answers revealed high conformity of practice within both categories of schools. There was a rather scattered pattern in the frequency with which schools assembled for common acts of worship.

Table 2:14

FREQUENCY OF SCHOOL ASSEMBLIES FOR COMMON ACTS
OF WORSHIP (PER CENT)

Frequency of meeting	Protestant			Catholic		
	Gr.	Sec.	Prim.	Gr.	Sec.	Prim.
Daily	90.9	81.8	67.3	60.0	72.7	34.2
Weekly	—	9.2	12.0	—	18.2	7.3
More than 10 times annually	—	4.5	1.7	—	—	4.8
3 to 10 times annually	—	—	10.4	—	9.1	22.0
1 to 2 times annually	—	—	5.2	—	—	12.3
Never	—	—	1.7	20.0	—	14.6
No response	9.1	4.5	1.7	20.0	—	4.8
TOTAL	100	100	100	100	100	100

Only 33 of the 65 responding Catholic schools (50.8 per cent) hold a daily act of worship. Such an assembly is more common at every level in Protestant than Catholic schools, which may reflect the statutory requirement on controlled schools to have a daily assembly. In fact 32 per cent of Protestant schools do not hold this required assembly each day.

On the other hand, virtually all children from the same school class attend common religious education classes (94.8 per cent) and there is little variation in pattern between Protestant and Catholic schools.

The number of pupils who opt out of religious studies sessions is very small. Only 14 out of the 141 schools which answered the question (9.9 per cent) have any pupils who did so. Twelve of these are Protestant schools.

In only one school does the number of pupils opting out of religious studies classes exceed 5 per cent.

Table 2:15

PUPILS WHO OPT OUT OF RELIGIOUS STUDIES
CLASSES (PER CENT)

Percentage of pupils opting out	Protestant			Catholic		
	Gr.	Sec.	Prim.	Gr.	Sec.	Prim.
0	36.35	59.1	72.4	40.0	95.4	80.5
less than 1	36.35	27.3	1.7	—	4.6	2.4
1–5	9.1	13.6	13.8	—	—	—
6–9	—	—	—	—	—	—
10–15	9.1	—	—	—	—	—
No response	9.1	—	12.1	60.0	—	17.1
TOTAL	100	100	100	100	100	100

Curricular and Extra-curricular activities

Teaching Practices

Contemporary discussion about the school curriculum often revolves around what are described as 'traditional' and 'progressive' teaching methods. While both these terms oversimplify the nature of the debate it was clearly important to measure the position of Protestant and Catholic schools along the progressive-traditional continuum. The operation of integrated studies and the use of streaming were selected as two indicators of a school's position on this continuum.

At primary school level a slightly higher proportion of Protestant (27.6 per cent) than Catholic (19.6 per cent) primary schools have adopted a degree of integration within the curriculum as expressed through the notion of the 'integrated day'. However, overall, this form of integration is not widely practised by the schools in the sample. Grammar schools in the sample report no integration at curriculum level, while secondary schools in both catergories operate some form of integration to precisely the same degree; exactly 45.5 per cent of both Protestant and Catholic secondary schools operate it for their lower forms only. Similarities between Protestant and Catholic secondary school organisation are also revealed in the general popularity of streaming classes. Exactly the same percentage (63.6 per cent) of schools in each category stream their pupils.

Use of Published Project Materials and Schools Broadcasts

The publication of teaching. packs, usually with project or thematic work in mind, has been a growing development in recent years. Many of these packs are multi-media in nature and provide a wide range of source material. In addition many of them have been created as part of the general 'curriculum reform' movement and, consequently, can be viewed as contributing to and reinforcing innovation at curriculum level. For the questionnaire a number of the more widely publicised of these packs were listed and schools asked to indicate if they used them.

Table 2:16
USE OF PROJECT MATERIALS (PER CENT)

Project materials	Protestant			Catholic		
	Gr.	Sec.	Prim.	Gr.	Sec.	Prim.
*Breakthrough to Literacy	—	—	24.1	—	—	29.1
Main Course of Study	—	13.6	—	—	4.5	4.1
*Schools Council Religious Education	—	—	24.1	—	—	4.9
†Schools Council Moral Education	—	40.9	—	18.2	31.8	—
†Schools Council Humanities Project	18.2	63.6	—	—	54.5	—
†Keele Integrated Studes	—	9.1	—	—	—	—

* Primary schools only   † Secondary schools only

It is rather difficult to draw any firm conclusion from these responses. Both school categories make use of such packs or kits. One of the most publicised and researched of these, the Schools Council Humanities Pack, and also the one which raises the problem of treating 'controversial issues' in the classroom, is more widely used in Protestant than in Catholic schools. On the other hand, it is interesting to note the extent to which the Schools Council Religious Education materials are reported to be used in Catholic schools in view of the fact that these have been developed with an inter-denominational and, even, a non-denominational audience in mind.

The *Breakthrough to Literacy* project was included in the list because of the integrated approach to literacy which it adopts whereby both reading and writing are developed side by side, drawing on the pupils' own linguistic experience in the initial stages. As symbolic of a creative approach to literacy it might be indicative of a 'progressive' trend in curricular practices. Both catergories use this project to a similar degree, with Catholic schools reporting a slightly higher level of usage.

Table 2:17

USE OF SCHOOLS BROADCASTS WITH NORTHERN IRISH CONTENT IN PRIMARY SCHOOLS (PER CENT)

Programme	Protestant	Catholic
'Today and Yesterday in Northern Ireland'	79.3	80.5
'Ulster in Focus'	62.1	51.2
Other broadcasts	48.3	34.1
No broadcasts	6.9	9.8

A range of school broadcasts which have a specifically Northern Irish content were listed for the primary schools to indicate if they used them. Results indicate that all the series listed are quite popular, though the television series *Ulster in Focus* is taken by fewer Catholic schools. There was a slightly higher percentage of Catholic schools taking no broadcasts.

Sport

Sport has been a very positive marker of difference between schools since games have acquired different cultural associations. In Northern Ireland these associations have traditionally been along lines which might broadly be defined as 'British' and 'Irish/Gaelic'. Indeed, the GAA (Gaelic Athletic Association) until quite recently had a rule prohibiting its members from playing association football (soccer), rugby football, hockey and cricket on the grounds that these were 'British' or 'foreign' games.

Table 2:18

SPORTS IN SCHOOLS (PER CENT)

Sport	Protestant			Catholic		
	Gr.	*Sec.*	*Prim.*	*Gr.*	*Sec.*	*Prim.*
Gaelic Football	—	—	—	60.0	63.6	53.7
Hurling	—	—	—	40.0	40.9	24.4
Camogie	—	—	—	40.0	50.0	7.3
Rugby	36.4	36.4	19.0	—	22.7	—
Cricket	36.4	45.5	—	—	—	—
Hockey	81.8	68.2	—	—	13.6	—
Soccer	9.1	81.8	65.5	20.0	45.5	34.1
Tennis	90.9	63.6	—	40.0	45.5	—
Netball	81.8	77.3	41.4	60.0	72.7	24.4
Basketball	45.5	77.3	—	80.0	63.3	—
Other	36.4	13.6	19.5	40.0	31.8	36.2

The wide range of sports practised in schools fall into three fairly clear groups. Gaelic football, hurling and camogie are not played in any Protestant schools. Rugby, cricket and hockey are popular in Protestant schools and markedly less popular in Catholic schools, although all of them, except cricket, were played to some extent. Equally notable, however, was a considerable number of sports which cut across the denominational split. These included, among others, association football (soccer), tennis, netball and basketball.

Visits

(a) Cultural Heritage:

Table 2:19

VISITS TO PLACES WITHIN NORTHERN IRELAND (PER CENT)

Place	Protestant			Catholic		
	Gr.	*Sec.*	*Prim.*	*Gr.*	*Sec.*	*Prim.*
Ulster Museum	45.5	45.5	34.5	60.0	45.5	12.2
Ulster Folk Museum	54.5	72.7	50.0	20.0	72.7	24.4
Ulster Transport Museum	9.1	36.4	22.4	20.0	22.7	9.8

Each category of school in the sample was surveyed for visits made to a number of places within the province and outside, and particularly to three places which might be referred to as of interest to the 'cultural heritage' of Ulster. Results indicate that secondary schools, perhaps as might be expected, tend to make more visits to such places than do primary schools, and also that the visits are equally common in both catergories. Only at primary level are Protestant schools more likely to visit these centres. When it comes to visits outside Northern Ireland, fewer Catholic than Protestant schools – 29.3 per cent against 46.6 per cent – make such tours. They are more popular in grammar schools than in secondary schools.

(b) Visits outside Northern Ireland

Table 2:20

VISITS TO PLACES OUTSIDE NORTHERN IRELAND (PER CENT)

Place	Protestant			Catholic		
	Gr.	*Sec.*	*Prim.*	*Gr.*	*Sec.*	*Prim.*
England and Wales	72.7	36.4	24.1	60.0	36.4	9.8
Scotland	45.5	31.8	27.6	60.0	31.8	7.3
Irish Republic	72.7	13.6	—	60.0	45.5	—
France	63.6	40.9	5.2	60.0	45.5	—
Other countries	72.7	72.7	8.6	20.0	72.7	7.3
No country	—	—	53.4	20.0	13.6	70.7

A higher proportion of Catholic schools make no visits at all to another country, but the similarities between the favoured venues indicates a considerable degree of shared cultural heritage between the two groups of schools.

There is considerable variety in the pattern of joint activities between schools in Northern Ireland, but they are much more common than shared facilities. Protestant grammar schools tend to display a stronger commitment to this practice than do any other kinds of schools in the sample. In general, Catholic schools appear to be less committed to joint enterprises than Protestant schools. A higher percentage of Catholic schools have no formal contact of this kind with other schools.

Table 2:21

SCHOOLS SHARING JOINT ACTIVITIES WITH OTHER SCHOOLS (PER CENT)

Joint Activities	Protestant			Catholic		
	Gr.	Sec.	Prim.	Gr.	Sec.	Prim.
Joint visits	36.4	9.1	12.1	20.1	9.0	9.8
Joint sports days	9.1	22.7	17.2	—	9.1	17.1
Joint concerts/plays	27.3	4.5	8.6	20.0	9.1	12.2
Joint church services	9.1	4.5	—	—	—	22.0
Joint carol services	27.3	9.1	6.9	20.0	9.1	14.6
Joint community action	45.5	13.6	—	40.0	9.1	—
Other joint activities	—	4.5	10.3	—	13.6	7.3
No formal contacts	—	36.4	24.1	20.0	36.4	34.1

Shared Facilities and Joint Activities

Sharing various kinds of facilities and activities provides an opportunity for schools to develop many kinds of contacts at staff and pupil levels. In this part of the questionnaire an attempt was made to discover to what extent, if any, secondary and grammar schools were in contact with other schools. No attempt was made to ascertain to what extent any sharing involves schools across both major categories.

Table 2:22

SECONDARY AND GRAMMAR SCHOOLS SHARING FACILITIES WITH OTHER SCHOOLS (PER CENT)

Shared facilities	Protestant		Catholic	
	Gr.	Sec.	Gr.	Sec.
Shared sixth form facilities	—	—	—	9.1
Shared science facilities	—	—	—	13.6
Shared personnel	27.3	9.1	40.0	13.6
Shared field centre	9.1	13.6	—	13.6
Shared library	—	—	—	4.5
Shared sports facilities	45.5	22.7	40.0	36.4

It is clear that the sharing of facilities is not widely practised in Northern Irish secondary and grammar schools, and that such sharing as does take place varies between categories of schools. Although the responses do not suggest any sharp general contrasts it is noteworthy that only in Catholic secondary schools does one find sharing with respect to sixth form, library and science facilities. This may be related to shortage of facilities.

All of these data can do little more than present a factual outline of practices within segregated schools. A questionnaire approach can provide little insight into either the actual results of these practices, or indeed the underlying influences which may have moulded them into their present form. For this reason, an attempt is made in subsequent chapters to communicate what it feels like actually to experience the social and cultural machinations of segregation. It might best be seen as a cameo of educational separation. Again it must be emphasised that no claim is made for the observed life in the two schools being generalisable in the statistical sense. My aspiration is simply that the observed phenomena and attendant interpretation might provide a clearer mirror in which we may view ourselves more objectively.

3

The Three Rs:
Religion, Ritual and Rivalry

THE quantitative data presented in Chapter 2 support the view that schools in Northern Ireland are polarised on religious grounds and that certain practices are peculiar to each. These data were accumulated by means of postal questionnaire and as such were removed from the reality of the everyday life in segregated schools. Such a research technique can do little more than present a broad general profile of segregation. It can contribute little to our knowledge of what it actually 'feels like' to live and serve in such a system. For this type of information it is essential that observation be carried out inside the schools themselves. However, detached or scientific observation and recording are inappropriate techniques in the study of these 'feelings'. The approach must be participant in the sense that one becomes as much as possible a member of the group or community being studied. This is not an easy task, but in order to gain insight into individual and group perceptions, one must become accepted by the individuals concerned as someone who understands their feelings and is prepared to defend them. This development in relationships takes time. For this reason, I spent one year full time in the schools – four months in St Judes, then four months in Rathlin followed by two further months in each. I taught class, took games, supervised, ate (and drank) with the staffs. In fact I did everything that they were expected to do.

Initially, observation was carried out across the whole spectrum of phenomena which comprise life in schools. No *a priori* limitations were imposed with regard to what counted as data. As the study developed the data seemed to fall within two broad parameters – 'school character' and 'school culture'.

There are, of course, many means by which a cultural analysis of a group or community may be carried out. In this study, two schools were selected because they were considered to represent cases or

49

examples of educational establishments which contributed to, and were influenced by, the two major cultural groups in Northern Ireland.

The aim, therefore, was to consider the two schools in the light of their cultural differences and ideologies and to employ this closely focussed study to better understand the cultural nuances existing in the community of Northern Ireland as a whole.

Mutual perceptions, representing as they do mutual realities, are another area of vital concern for any study attempting to illuminate the culture of Northern Irish schools. The data collected in attempting to describe the ethos of both schools is presented under two broad headings. These headings have a specific meaning, and as such require definition and elaboration.

Character

This aspect of the schools is seen to be governed by influences acting within a school or exerted by individuals who have a direct concern for that school. In this context the principal is seen to have a central role in the character of the school. His personality and views on management will profoundly affect the day to day running of his 'domain'. The channels of communication which exist between himself and his staff are significantly influenced by his personality and approach.

More concrete factors contribute to the character of any school. Its geographical position, the physical state of its buildings, resources, the social class structure of its immediate environment and the social class backgrounds of staff may all generate a unique character of a school.

It may seem erroneous, with so many factors and influences operating, to describe any school as having one, unique character. Certainly all the individuals involved will perceive the school in an ideosyncratic manner and as such there may be as many characteristic realities as there are perceptions of them. However, the extent to which these perceptions and meanings are shared, or at least negotiated, is seen as the major factor in the construction of a unique character for a school.

Culture

Any cultural analysis in Northern Ireland must take into account the peculiar position that schools occupy in that area. Religion, politics and culture are almost inextricably enmeshed. In general, Protestants subscribe to a Unionist political ideology and maintain their own cultural traditions, attitudes, values and behaviours which are largely a function of an English or Scottish identity. Catholics, on the other hand, aspire, to varying degrees, towards a Nationalist ideal and possess a set of values and traditions emantating from, and identifying with, an Irish heritage. This distinction, however, is necessarily and intentionally both synoptic and stark and as such may be subject to specific criticism. It is employed simply to provide broad parameters which helped initial structuring of observation within the schools.

It is important to restate that primary schools in Northern Ireland are either Protestant or Catholic. Official nomenclature or rhetoric does nothing to soften this fact. Controlled/state schools are attended almost exclusively by Protestant pupils who are taught by Protestant teachers. Maintained schools reflect an even greater degree of polarisation, especially at primary level, where almost without exception they are populated by Catholic teachers and pupils.

Indeed, in the maintained primary sector there is almost an institutional veto against the employment of non-Catholic teachers, since in order to qualify to teach there one requires a religious instruction certificate which is specifically Catholic in nature and design.

Thus two basic conclusions can be drawn about society in Northern Ireland. Firstly, one's religion is very closely related to cultural membership and, secondly, schools exist as religiously polarised institutions serving each major cultural group. These conclusions are neither original nor dramatic. What is rather more contentious is whether they are perceived in terms of cause or effect. That is, do segregated schools cause social divisiveness or, does the existence of disparate cultural groups in society dictate the co-existence of segregated education?

Those kinds of question prompted an in-depth cultural analysis of two schools in Northern Ireland (one Catholic, St Judes, the other Protestant, Rathlin) which considered the extent to which they might be seen to contribute to, or be influenced by, the religio/cultural group which considered each school to belong to it. It is this aspect of school life which is termed the *culture* of the school.

Behaviour, then, seen in terms of culture, infers uniformity and consensus with other schools of similar traditional and religious identities. No two schools, on the other hand, will have identical *character*. When these terms appear in the text they should be interpreted in the light of the specific definitions attributed to them above.

It is not being suggested, however, that human behaviour can be located exclusively under either heading or that no overlap occurs between them. Indeed such 'grey areas' are discussed in the text. The bipartite format simply reflects an attempt to dissect and analyse the unidimensional concept of 'ethos' which has been more generally applied in descriptions of Protestant and Catholic schools in Northern Ireland.

The most immediate impressions formed by a stranger entering a school are engendered by the symbols displayed and the rituals enacted within it. It is on the basis of such stimuli, therefore, that this particular study of the culture and character of the schools commences. Despite the fact that in many cases such stimuli are obvious, it should not be assumed that they provide superficial information only. The rituals and symbols themselves are merely the instruments through which deeper value positions are conveyed and to which meanings are apportioned.

A symbol is defined as an object which is displayed to evoke images and meanings designed to influence attitudes and values and thus structure behaviour. In this sense ritual is also a symbol, but is more active and participatory. It implies the involvement and identification of members of the group for which it has specific meaning. In the case of schools these meanings may be communicated to, or understood by, members of a particular school only. In which case they can be said to preserve the character of the school.

Such a case was demonstrated by the yearly pageant in Rathlin which highlighted different aspects of the school's long historic past. Pride was expressed in its tradition, and children were made aware of the distinctiveness of the school, which dates back to the plantation of Ireland. The pageant concluded with the rousing musical exhortation, 'Let's be proud of our story and our past glory'. In the dim assembly hall parents, many of whom were past pupils, clasped hands with their enraptured offspring. There was an almost tangible feeling of belonging to a sentimentally exclusive fellowship.

Symbols in schools, however, can have meaning for a much larger group who may have no direct contact or relationship with that particular school. The 6 x 2½ ft papal flag hanging in St Judes is a case in point. A Roman Catholic entering St Judes, even though he had never done so before, will immediately be made aware that the school is part of a more general system of which he has had experience. He can, therefore, proceed to operate on the assumption that both the religious and cultural values which he himself holds will be reflected and cherished within that school. Symbols, therefore, can stimulate subsequent behaviour.

Such 'cues' are important in Northern Ireland, where at any gathering members will assiduously attempt to determine the religious affiliation and hence political and cultural aspirations of the others. There is nothing insidious in this process, it is simply a means of avoiding possible embarrassment. The more visible the symbols displayed, the more this identification process is facilitated.

There is, however, another significant outcome which such overt symbols may precipitate. Protestants entering St Judes and being confronted by the papal flag – or indeed Catholics observing the large Union Jack outside Rathlin (both are of equal cultural and religious significance) – may well have their stereotypes of the other type of school confirmed. These stereotypes are, by definition, based on superficial observation or hearsay evidence. In Rathlin, Ms Jackson, who taught P4, confided in me:

> When I saw all those statues and things in St Judes it made me wonder just what exactly went on there.

In St Judes, Mr White was more outspoken:

> They fly the flag down there (in Rathlin) to show that they are more British than the British themselves. It's also to let us know that they are the lords and masters and we should be continually aware of it. I wonder what would happen if we tried to fly the tricolour?

These observations demonstrate well the dangers of symbols in a segregated society. Individuals who are not aware of the meaning structures of those for which the symbols are constructed must interpret their display at a superficial level. Rituals and symbols, by their very nature, must be clearly visible. In Northern Ireland, however, visibility can be perceived as provocation.

In St Judes, for instance, members would go to any lengths to avoid giving offence, yet they considered it quite natural to display 'statues and things' in a Catholic school. In Rathlin, many of the teachers were unaware that the Union Jack fluttered daily outside their school – and in fact could not have cared less if it did or not. They also found it quite incomprehensible that a state school, in the United Kingdom, flying the British emblem, could cause offence:

> If they (Catholics) want to stay out, well that's fine with us. But how can they object to us showing that we want to stay in?

These comments, and many more on the same topic, suggest that more cognisance is taken of symbols by those who are observing them than by those who consciously or otherwise are displaying them. Why then do such symbols and rituals continue to exist?

In order to answer this question adequately one must consider rituals and symbols from four main aspects: the symbols and ritualistic practices themselves; the intention of those presenting the rituals and symbols; those for whom they are constructed and presented; observers who are not familiar with the meaning structures of the rituals and symbols.

Symbols and Rituals within the School

The choice and presentation of books was seen to be symbolic of what each school was trying to do. Research on this topic has been carried out in Northern Irish schools by Magee (1970), Fulton (1973) and Farren (1976). The thrust of such research has been the place and nature of what might be described as academic literature – mathematics, geography, and more especially, history.

In this study, however, it was considered more appropriate to study what might (perhaps unfairly) be described as peripheral reading, i.e. library books and those collections in surrounding classrooms which have been built up over the years by the teachers.

However, with regard to academic books one observation warrants inclusion: in St Judes, over half of this type of literature was ordered through publishers in Dublin (mainly the Educational Company). In Rathlin, on the other hand, this publisher's catalogue was not present in the school nor did anyone know of its existence. In fact, only one book – *The Living Past* – published by the Educational Company in Dublin was requested by Rathlin and eventually used by pupils in the school. The principal, Mr Long, was quite enthusiastic about the book but he encountered strong opposition from some staff, based to some extent on the fact that in the book post office boxes were green (as they are in the Republic of Ireland) and that the words 'Parochial Hall' appeared on the first page!

One teacher, Mr McDowell, told me that he had become interested in Irish history as a result of several holidays in Donegal. He had always been aware of a gulf in his knowledge of the history and geography of Ireland as a whole:

> You see, I was brought up in a Protestant area and received all my education in state schools. You just were not taught anything about the south of Ireland. . . Australia and New Zealand, yes, because they were part of the Commonwealth. But the south of Ireland just didn't exist in state schools. Things are changing a bit now because 'The Troubles' have forced us to try to understand what is going on.

These comments suggest that formal curricula in state schools are English or British orientated almost to the exclusion of Irish studies. This in fact is reinforced by the research cited previously.

An attempt was made in this respect to determine if books which were present in the schools, but which the pupils had the choice of reading, might also demonstrate differing cultural orientations in St Judes and Rathlin.

One structural difference between the two schools was that Rathlin had a recognised library room while St Judes did not. Both used the services of the mobile library which visited the schools regularly. Individual teachers obtained a supply of books from this source and retained these in their classrooms. There was a marked difference in essence and tenor between the literature available for reading by the pupils in the two schools. For the purpose of comparison the books are described under the three main headings of religious, factual and fictional.

In general the religious books in Rathlin were of a biblical nature. There were over forty books on biblical stories in the library. These were all well-thumbed and taken home on many occasions. There were, however, two conspicuous exceptions, *Maps of Monastic Ireland* and *Ignatius Loyola and the Jesuits*. While both of these texts may have been read in the library itself, not one child in the school had ever availed of the facility, encouraged by the school, of taking the books home to read. There were also copies of the Bible (the New English version) in every classroom. In other classrooms *Stories from the Bible* and *The Bible for Children* were typical texts. Other books which were deemed to be of a religious nature were in the main historical accounts of the Christian church in Europe and Britain – *The Church Marches On* was one such text. In the music teacher's room there was a copy of *The Daily Service: Prayers and Hymns for Schools* (Northern Ireland edition). Interestingly, this edition was authorised by the Boards of Education of the Presbyterian, Methodist and Church of Ireland churches only.

In St Judes, religious texts of all types abounded. They were all, however, specifically Catholic in nature and there were examples in every classroom. The books varied from academic – *Religious Teaching in Catholic Schools* – to almost proselytising literature. For example, Mrs White explained that she purposely left magazines such as *The Far East* and *Africa,* both missionary publications, lying around the classroom because 'You never know when they might spark off a vocation'. Here then is an example of Catholic schools adopting a vocational role in a more specific sense than when the term is more generally applied to schools, i.e. an aspiration to produce future priests. This was reinforced at the school mass, where the children were exhorted to consider becoming 'the teachers and priests of the future'.

In St Judes there existed a selection of books which would seem to symbolise a religio/geographic attachment with Rome. Many texts of this type were observed in several senior classrooms in the school: *The Vatican and Sistine Chapel; A Visitor to Rome; Roma Photographs; The Eternal City* were typical. In fact there were more books about Rome in the school than there were about Belfast. This range of books in the Catholic school obviously reflected an awareness of, and identity with, its religious epicentre.

If there was a religio/cultural identification with Rome suggested by the para-religious literature in St Judes, then there was just as clear a politico/cultural attachment with the city of London exhibited in Rathlin.

It is of interest that both schools presented strong evidence suggesting cultural attachments with locations outside the country in which they were situated. This same trend was demonstrated by geography and history books which formed the bulk of the casual reading in classrooms and the library. In Rathlin the vast majority of such books were strongly British in content. Books such as *The Plague and Fire of London, Gunpowder Plot, Warwick John and Magna Carta, The Crusade, Great Men and Women from Britain's Past, Norman Britain, Roman Britain, The Book of London, Come to London* and *This is London* were typical of a British influence of a type which was simply not available in St Judes.

In the latter school the bulk of such books tended to emphasise an all-Ireland or Nationalist culture – *O'Connell, Man and Boy, The Republic of Ireland, Ancient History of Ireland, Tales of Irish Enchantment, The Charm of Ireland, Irish Myth and Magic, Ireland from Old Photographs,* were typical of the literature surrounding every classroom in the school. All of these books treated Ireland as a unit of thirty-two counties rather than recognising the six counties of Northern Ireland as being a separate entity.

At a symbolic level, therefore, the casual literature in both schools seemed to encourage the cherishing of cultures which had their roots outside Northern Ireland itself. This may well make these two cultures all the more incompatible, since they have little in common geographically, historically or traditionally. Symbols within schools which can be identified with one culture may well be anathema to members of the other, thus further highlighting the separateness of the two educational systems.

Apart from books there were many other rituals and symbols which seemed to exist to identify members as a distinct collectivity (character) or to encourage broader cultural affiliation.

The character of Rathlin was strongly academic in orientation, and ritual tended to acclaim and reinforce such a rationale. Several teachers commented on this aspect of the school, such as Ms Thompson, a P4 teacher:

> The emphasis here is on competition in every field. You have to be tops in everything. This results in the long term aim of the school being a drive to succeed. Prize day is a good example of this

competition idea. It leads to the equation, Rathlin = cut throat = parents get caught up = prizes for best = watches for very best.

Two of my children got watches (for head boy and head girl). I was mortified standing there since many of the children struggled hard and got nothing except 20p for standing in line! It's all a bit pathetic.

However, there were other points of view, such as that of Ms Walker, P7:

In all fields of endeavour, achievement is rewarded, so why not in schools? In any case all the children get 20p. The children don't feel neglected but rather look back on prize day with affection.

Prize day itself was steeped in pomp and tradition, with the robed platform party proceeding to an elevated stage in a nearby church hall. Those attending were left in no doubt by the principal with regard to the purpose of the occasion:

Prize day is a reminder of the academic success and standards of the school. . . I am happy to report that I think our academic standard is as high as ever. This is reflected in the list of prizewinners.

And indeed it was, with nine out of the ten prizes for each class being awarded for academic achievement and one awarded for 'helpfulness'.

The impression was clearly given that prize day was the most important day of the year and that the success which was publicly acclaimed there should be the aspiration of every pupil in the school. The ritual, therefore, existed as both recognition of success and an incentive for the younger pupils to comply and identify with the intentions of the school.

Several of the staff were self-conscious about prize day itself and its attendant meanings. When it became known that I had been invited to the ceremony, teacher reaction was almost universal: 'You'll fill your notebook tomorrow' and,' Don't be too hard on us, it's all for show really' were typical comments.

In fact some years ago there existed a lobby within the school to discontinue the event, or at least to distribute prizes for a broader range of abilities. This point of view was defeated, however, and now prize day has been established as an immutable tradition which publicly acclaims the academic achievement of pupils and hence the success of the school.

The head boy and girl are also chosen soley on academic criteria. The two who excel most in this domain in their final year at the school are chosen. This in fact means that by the time they are awarded the acclaim, and have had their names added to the role of honour on a plaque in the main corridor, they have in fact left school. This 'posthumous beatification' has important implications. Since the recipients are acclaimed *in absentia,* they cannot obviously be expected to carry out any specific duties within the school. Their appointment does, however, give a clear indication about the values which are held dear by the school.

But what of the other pupils who are not so successful? One teacher informed me that she had often noticed that the head boy and girl had been among the most popular pupils. If this is so, and other teachers agreed that it was, it might be that their popularity may be due in part to the fact that they epitomise all that the school extols and encourages. Other pupils, having been continually made aware of the attributes which distinguish an ideal pupil, may as a result identify with such attributes and with pupils who are publicly revered for having them in abundance.

From observation of, and brief discussions with, pupils it did not seem to matter if most of them were not endowed with academic ability. They could at least bask in the reflected glory of those who were.

> My mummy says that this is the best school in. . . . They make you work hard here so that you are better than anyone else when you get to secondary school.

This comment was made by a boy who was considered by the teacher to be the 'weakest' pupil in P7. It would suggest that the school had succeeded in making an academic emphasis appealing even to those who were unsuccessful with this facet of education.

Ritual has played a major role in this process. Prize day, for example, and its framework of meanings gives a clear indication of what the institution is trying to do. It also serves to encourage a sharing of these intentions by individuals directly involved with the school. In other words, it proclaims and perpetuates one facet of the character of the school.

The occasion also had strong cultural undertones. In the first place the platform party was composed of establishment figures; the management committee, the chief officer of the Education and Library Board, ministers of the three major Protestant groups and representatives of the body who had founded the school. All of these represented successful members of the cultural group to which the pupils belonged.

Proceedings commenced with a request by the principal that, 'To show our loyalty, let's sing our National Anthem [God Save the Queen]', which was complied with, with gusto. He also ended his yearly report with the claim,

> It is a great honour to wear the motto of the City of [a major English city] on our uniform. We do so with much pride.

These two examples of action within Rathlin were perfectly natural recognitions of a shared cultural identity in the school. They served to bind the members as part of a broad (i.e. British) community but also to emphasise the school's distinctiveness in terms of its unusually close links with Britain.

While one might expect the latter function to differ from all other schools, it must be emphasised that neither aspect would ever be enacted in St Judes, nor indeed in any Catholic achool, where members lack any such affinity with either monarchy or the site of such rule. This may seem a gross over-generalisation, but it is one that can be made with justification. It is in fact generally accepted in Northern Ireland that Protestants cling to a British identity and Roman Catholics to a vaguely nationalistic/Catholic ideal.

In fact, formal ritual within St Judes tended to emphasise religious identity, and monthly mass was the most powerful instance of this. Here, emphasis was placed on the strong bond that should exist between church, parents and school. The church was the unifying factor among all Catholic schools. Such ritual, therefore, in the school, in emphasising this global collectivity, could be said to be predominantly cultural in content. The pupils were being made aware that they were members of a much larger family:

> May God our Father bless the families, teachers and the priests in this parish as they hand on the faith to the children. . . May the Holy Spirit guide our hearts and strengthen our wills so that we may all grow as one family of God.

This relationship between church and school was constantly reinforced. The instructions for the offertory procession of one mass demonstrate the point:

. . . Parents, teachers and pupils could form an offertory procession bringing bread and wine, flowers, some symbols of school work, e.g. books, etc. . .

All religious ceremonies and rituals proceeded during school time – mass, first communion, confirmation, confessions, etc. all took place in the adjoining church during school hours. The school closed for all major church holidays, a fact which seemed to provide the most graphic evidence to the pupils of both schools that 'the other school was different'.

Less public were the internal religious symbols and rituals, such as the parish priest visiting the school every year to distribute ashes to pupils and teachers on Ash Wednesday, or classes stopping for prayer as the angelus bell, which could be heard clearly from the parish church fifty yards away, pealed out dolefully every day at twelve o'clock. This action tended to emphasise both the physical and religious affinity of church and school. The rota of altar boys for parish mass was posted on the main school notice board. Prayers and church announcements were made at assembly. All of these served to highlight the natural and integral presence of Catholicism within the school.

This concept, which is central to the argument for the retention of the Catholic school system, was also stressed within the formal curriculum. Preparation for first communion formed part of religious instruction classes (and in fact many other classes as the event grew more imminent!). Religious education was in fact the teaching of Catholic doctrine. There was none of the ambivalence or generality in this respect which was observed in Rathlin and demanded by the 1930 Education Act in state schools.

Further evidence of the church/school link was observed in Ms Elder's classroom. During the month of May a small altar was introduced which consisted of flowers which the children brought in daily and a large statue of the Virgin Mary. Surrounding these symbols were pupil essays about the Blessed Virgin which had been marked and graded in the normal way.

All of these demonstrations not only highlight the links between church and school but also confirm the catholicity of the school itself. This fact has political and cultural ramifications. Apart altogether from the historic Catholic connection with Nationalism, the fact that Catholicism is emphasised within their schools inevitably allies them with Catholic Ireland. In reality this means the Republic of Ireland and ideally, perhaps, a united Ireland. In other words, the emphasis on Catholicism may be seen, and in fact certainly is seen, as a political acclamation. Thus while the Catholic hierarchy may defend their schools on religious grounds, many Protestants, including the staff in Rathlin, perceived them to be strongly political in nature. Every ritual and symbol observed or heard about in Catholic schools reinforces this perception.

Here, then, is another example of why it is important that ritual should not be taken lightly. It is on the basis of such stimuli, and the meanings which are attributed to them, that much social action is constructed.

While ritual in St Judes can be seen to reflect a national identity cloaked perhaps in the mantle of religion, no such ambiguity was observed in Rathlin's demonstration of a British affiliation. Here ritual at a cultural level was visibly and self-avowedly British. As already noted, the emblem of Britain is flown daily outside the school. State schools in the area are required by the local Education and Library Board to display this symbol. Such a formal requirement would seem to suggest an official desire either publicly to affirm the link with Britain or consciously to influence the attitudinal positions of pupils within. It would seem that neither of these intentions will facilitate a Catholic acceptance of the official claim that state schools are open to all and thus already integrated. They are perceived to advocate a cultural position which is anathema to the majority of Catholics.

Less visible to outsiders were the internal symbols and rituals in Rathlin which also emphasised a British culture. A 5 x 5 ft memorial plaque was affixed in the P6 classroom on which were named all the past pupils of the school who had fought in the 'Two Great Wars', some of whom had made the ultimate sacrifice. These men had fought in defence of the country of the present pupil population, i.e. Britain, and were being honoured for doing so. Thus the emblem provided an example of a symbol which constructs a framework of meaning over and beyond its objective self. It evokes a sympathy and empathy with others who had striven to maintain the security of the cultural group to which the pupils also belonged.

At a more superficial, though no less influential, level all the pupils in the school received Jubilee coins to commemorate the first twenty-five years of Queen Elizabeth's reign. Significantly, the Jubilee celebrations received only ridicule in St Judes.

Cultural identity, however, would hardly be constructed, or indeed significantly influenced, by any one symbol or ritual. It is rather the cumulative effect of the myriad of such stimuli which may affect the attitudes and hence behaviour of pupils. The impact is likely to be greater the more public and consensual the stimuli. That is, the more members of the social group who actively take part in it. Special assemblies in Rathlin provide a good example of this.

On Commonwealth Day, the whole of assembly was devoted to this topic. A letter from the queen was read out to the pupils by Mr Long. He also delivered a brief eulogy about the commonwealth. One of the ministers present gave a homily about the queen and the good works she carried out for her subjects. The proceedings closed with everyone singing a verse of 'God Save the Queen'. Assembly broke up amid a festive atmosphere. All pupils from P1 to P7 were united with teachers and clergy in a common identity within a commonwealth family.

While this particular aspect of social action within Rathlin seemed both natural and enjoyable, it is inconceivable that anything comparable would ever be enacted in St Judes. When I described the ritual to staff there, it was treated with derision. The general feeling was articulated by Ms Elder:

> What has the great commonwealth ever done for us? British colonialists have milked Ireland dry for centuries and yet you still get people who applaud them for it. I think they are mad or stupid. In Rathlin they get people coming every year and dishing out a few prizes to the natives and they are treated like God Almighty. . . Have they no pride at all? God, it's pathetic!

The general intensity of reaction in St Judes was impressive. It demonstrated graphically the perceptual and cultural gulf that existed between the two establishments, and very probably between the two separate systems of schooling operating in Northern Ireland as a whole.

What has been considered thus far with regard to the cultural and characteristic experience of individuals within the two schools is the formal, traditional and consensual rituals and symbols presented there. In addition to these, another factor was observed to be of significance in this context.

The behaviour of staff in groups or as individuals can be regarded as giving cues to other individuals or groups in an organisation or community. March (1965), for example, has written of the importance of traditions, roles, values and norms that are part of life in organisations. He claims that much behaviour therein is influenced by participants' awareness of these mental states and by pressures generated by others who are influenced by these states. More specifically, Sockett (1979) has written about schools in Northern Ireland:

> The function of the school in the political matrix is different, quite different from the kind of (public) stance schools adopt. A school can quite well 'stand' as an 'oasis' in a sea of troubles, while sumultaneously propagating sets of attitudes in the official curriculum and goodness knows what in the unofficial curriculum which runs absolutely counter to its formal 'oasis' position.

There were examples in both schools of how such sets of attitudes might have been propagated by the spontaneous action and comment of teachers. It was interesting that many more examples of this type were recorded in St Judes. This may well be indicative of a methodological difficulty of carrying out comparative research in a sensitive area. Perhaps such spontaneity almost by definition represents unguarded or extemporaneous action and comment. The staff in St Judes, being aware that I was a fellow Catholic, and therefore assuming that I subscribed to value positions similar to their own, felt less constrained to avoid offence. The opposite may have applied in Rathlin.

On one occasion in St Judes both P1 classes were watching a video recording of a schools programme on television. As the programme finished the tape continued running to display a sports programme which presumably had been recorded some time earlier. The sports commenced with the playing of the British national anthem. As soon as it became clear what the music was, both teachers ran forward shrieking and laughing to switch the television off. This action was greeted with laughter and some applause from the pupils. It should be noted that many of these pupils were less than five years old, which may give some credence to the claim by several teachers in St Judes that the attitudes of the children are formed at home. It hardly confirms the other claims by these teachers that the school has a minimal effect on the attitudes of pupils. Such cues, delivered by individuals whom these young children hold in high esteem, must have a major influence on how they will react when confronted with similar symbols in the future.

Another example of this kind of jocular derision occurred in a P5 classroom in which I was observing. The news that Princess Anne had given birth to a baby boy had just broken and the topic arose during the class. The teacher exclaimed, 'Oh no, not another one!' (Laughter) 'He'll not have to worry about the electricity bill.' (Laughter) 'Did he have a silver spoon in his mouth?' (Explanation of what the term meant and return to normal work.) Again this interlude seemed to form a bond between the teacher and the *whole* class. Everyone shared in this general identity. For a few brief moments the class was a unit. It would seem, therefore, that this type of influence may be all the more powerful since it takes place in an atmosphere of solidarity between teacher and pupils which is rarely, if ever, achieved in daily classroom life.

This commonality of response was by no means a prerequisite for cultural messages and signals to be transferred. On poppy day a representative called at St Judes with a supply of the emblems (symbols?) and a pupil sold these around the school. My first reaction to this was one of surprise. I had not expected either an acceptance or display of poppies (with their British connotations) in a Catholic school. This is indicative of the danger of a participant researcher failing to bracket his preconceptions and expectations. However, as it transpired I was half right! While many of the pupils wore the poppies not one teacher did. This did not appear to be an unwillingness to support the charity since most of them contributed, but rather that they did not wish to be seen to support it. This mute affirmation must surely have been noticed and noted by the pupils.

In discussion with the staff later several of them expressed the view that they would experience a kind of atavistic unease if they were to wear a poppy. But they did suggest that the fact that poppies were sold in the school demonstrated how liberal St Judes was. This same self-perceived liberalism was observed on another occasion. The Royal

Ulster Constabulary visited the school to give lessons to the children on the highway code. While several members of the staff expressed an animosity towards the visitors they still gave the impression that the fact that they had been allowed in at all showed how broad-minded their establishement was!

One further example of an individual member of staff attempting to manipulate cultural consensus where in fact none had previously existed was observed in Mr White's class. It was during the soccer season, and Northern Ireland had been drawn against the Republic of Ireland in a qualifying round of a major competiton. The event arose in the course of class conversation. It seemed that most of the boys in the class supported Northern Ireland. Their teacher reacted by exclaiming, 'What do you want to support *them* for?' Quite obviously, for Mr White, Northern Ireland was the opposition and the Republic or Ireland was the home team.

To a visiting 'guru' this ideal of an affinity with the Republic of Ireland seemed on occasion to be taken to quite absurd lengths. A child in St Judes asked his teacher if the class could go on an outing to the Ulster Folk Museum. His teacher replied that he could not understand why they should want to go there since 'there is nothing there which shows our true heritage'. It would seem paradoxical that antipathy towards one part of the country transcended his broader nationalistic ideals.

It is interesting, however, that this identity with the Republic of Ireland is assumed by outsiders to exist in Catholic schools and indeed can be capitalised upon. The principal of St Judes entered the staffroom and announced that although the school had already its complement of student teachers on teaching practice for the year, he had decided to accept another two. Part of the reason for this was that he had been informed by Mr Bates (the lecturer in the teacher training college responsible for student placement) that the two were from Donegal in the Republic of Ireland. I spoke to Mr Bates afterwards and he informed me that he unashamedly emphasised origins in such cases because 'it greatly enhances their chances of being accepted in Catholic schools'. He also stated that he would not mention their geographical background if he was attempting to place them in state schools. It must also be said, however, that since the two were from Donegal it could be, and was, assumed that they were also Catholic.

The Intentions of the Presenters

This section attempts to analyse the perceived purpose of the individuals and groups who were presenting and perpetuating rituals and symbols. It is perhaps a truism to suggest that the purpose of these presenters is to influence attitudes and values of the children within the schools and thus structure subsequent behaviour. This may well emanate from a perception of their occupational task. One facet of this task was to prepare and develop children academically, for which the 'eleven plus' examination (taken by children in their final year at primary school) in itself offered ritual certification. This aspiration was shared by those teaching in Rathlin and those in St Judes and resulted in a unity of process common to both schools. In this context, the general overt curricular practices were so similar, that the thrust of the research was directed towards other aspects of schooling which might shed light on, and thus aid comprehension of, the two segregated systems which hitherto have tended to be discussed at a superficial and relatively ill-informed level. It must be emphasised, therefore, that any differences between the two schools discussed in this section, or indeed the book as a whole, should be viewed in the light of the very many practices and procedures which were common to both.

In St Judes there seemed to be a clear purpose in the employment of ritual, i.e. to emphasise the catholicity of the church/home/school trinity. This aspiration was demonstrated by action throughout the whole school, and was as obvious to an outside observer as it was taken for granted by the school members. Implicit in this emphasis on the values of the Catholic home and school was the reinforcement of a Nationalist culture and identity.

In Rathlin there seemed to be more ambivalence in this respect. While there were rituals and symbols presented which accentuated a broad Protestant (or British) identity, there appeared to be a greater concern for demonstrating that their school was unique and in fact better than any other within the general state system.

As observation proceeded it became apparent that in St Judes, rituals and symbols existed predominately to emphasise the *culture* of the school. In Rathlin, such activities seemed mainly designed to demonstrate the distinctive *character* of the institution. This may well be explained by the differing rationales of the two establishments – a point which will be elaborated upon later.

Those for whom Rituals and Symbols are Constructed

The case for children attending St Judes is clear; quite simply it is the local Catholic school in the area. Parents send their children there because they have made the moral decision that their children should be brought up as Catholics. The more visible evidence that exists within the school that it is striving towards this end then the less conflict there will be between parent and school. Ritual then serves to bind these people into a community. Their meaning is clear and their purpose accepted.

Although Rathlin is a Protestant school (all staff are Protestant and only six pupils are Catholic) it is not homogenously so. One factor which unites the vast majority of Protestants in Northern Ireland is a claim to be British (Robinson (1971); Russell (1972)). This aspect of schooling was evident in Rathlin and other state schools which I visited. Rathlin, however, has a longer history and tradition than most. It was founded in the eighteenth century by a group of people who were appalled by the 'lack of learning' in the area. It has striven over the years to establish an individual or unique character based on academic excellence.

The success rate in the 'eleven plus' examination is 20 per cent above the national average. This statistic itself becomes a symbol which communicates meanings to parents of prospective pupils about what the institution is trying to do. Rathlin, therefore, has an appeal for a section of the community who value academic emphasis in schools. This appeal is reinforced by rituals within the school where the head boy and girl are appointed solely on academic criteria and by the most powerful ritual observed in either school, prize day, where the overwhelming majority of prizes are awarded for academic achievement.

It is not being suggested that such symbols were the sole determinant of pupil composition in Rathlin. Certainly it was attended by children living in the immediate area. However, it is no coincidence that the school is described by its principal as 'more middle-class than most' although it is sited in a working-class area and the offspring of parents from the professional classes in the town are disproportionately represented.

The vice-principal of Rathlin, who was appointed in the same year as my observation was carried out, described this feeling of distinctiveness:

> When I applied for the job I did so with my tongue in my cheek not really expecting to get it. When I was offered the post I began in earnest to make enquiries about the place. I became really apprehensive about taking up the post because of the name (i.e. the very high reputation) that the school had in the area.

This, then, was the perception of the school held by people who had some knowledge of it, based largely, it seemed, on the more obvious signs (or symbols) of standards and results, but also on the tradition and ritual which contributed to its public image.

It can be argued, therefore, that rituals and symbols are important not only for individuals within an institution/school but also for prospective members who are attempting to determine which institution might best reflect and encourage their own attitudes and values.

Observers who are not familiar with the Meaning Structures of the Rituals and Symbols

Rathlin, being a state school, is legally non-denominational. It is, however, attended almost exclusively by Protestants who acclaim Unionist or British aspirations. The school therefore, in common with other state schools, is placed in the invidious position of attempting to reflect or reinforce the values and attitudes of a broadly Unionist culture while at the same time avoiding being seen as exclusively Protestant. The Union Jack flying outside Rathlin provides a good example of this dilemma. When considered at all, the staff there considered that it was perfectly natural to have such an emblem in a school which was located in the United Kingdom. One teacher articulated the mood:

> I don't know why you are making such a fuss about the flag. Why should we apologise for flying it? We are a state school and the flag is the emblem of the state. (Laughing) Would you rather we flew the tricolour or the hammer and sickle?

The fact that I had neither been 'making a fuss' nor suggesting that apologies were required, and the defensive tone used, suggested that the teacher was aware that possible offence could be taken by the exhibiton of the emblem. In fact it is true to say that, in general, and certainly among the staff in St Judes, Catholics equate the Union Jack with Britishness and, therefore, Protestantism. This reality for them, therefore, is that Rathlin is a Protestant school.

The principal and staff in Rathlin vehemently denied any such assertion. They claimed (rightly) that their school was open to all. However, every ritual and symbol which demonstrated their natural British aspirations simultaneously reinforced the Catholic conviction that state schools were Protestant establishments and actively sought to maintain an exclusively Protestant nature. This perception can lead to quite extreme positions being adopted. Shortly before I arrived, the parish priest of St Judes refused to allow the school choir to partake in a musical festival which was taking place in a local town hall simply because the Union Jack was flying outside. His reason, given to the staff, was:

> If they (Protestants) make it clear that we are not welcome, then why should we disappoint them?

The fact that none of the other choirs had any responsibility for the display of the symbol nor, it would seem, would the vast majority have noticed its absence, is irrelevant. The point is that, for the parish priest at least, meanings were attached to the object so that it was seen as a provocation. This, then, was the reality of the situation as far as St Judes was concerned, and social behaviour, in the form of a boycott, ensued. The teacher who had previously mentioned to me that she 'wondered what went on in Catholic schools' elaborated on this point in a later discussion:

> We play St Judes often in games and we visit their school regularly. I never fail to be impressed by the plethora of religious pictures and icons staring at you around every corner. It's hard to escape the view that a special show is being put on for our benefit. . . this doesn't just apply to St Judes, of course, but they must know that these are the very things that we have objections to yet still they are flaunted everywhere.

I asked what this 'special show' might be for.

> Oh, I think to demonstrate their separateness and isolation from the state system of education. . . I suppose this might be fair enough but

in general in Northern Ireland I think that Catholics don't want to have anything to do with the state. That's why they are so against integrated education.

There are three interesting conclusions which can be drawn from these remarks. Firstly, the speaker's perception that the symbols were offensive to teachers from state schools at a religious level and thus demonstrated Catholic rejection of the 'state system of education' would seem to suggest that she accepted that the state system was in fact Protestant in composition.

Secondly, that the rejection of state education by Catholics was seen in terms of opposition to integrated education would seem to suggest that in her opinion the two were synonomous (integrated education entailed Catholic schools joining the state system).

Finally, and perhaps of most import for this section, is that implied in the comments is a perception of *intent* to cause offence in the 'flaunting' of religious symbols, thus representing a disloyalty to a system which she considered both natural and proper.

Here, then, are examples of symbols being misinterpreted by individuals for whom they were not constructed. I put Ms Jackson's views and other similar ones of Rathlin teachers to the staff in St Judes. They reacted unanimously to the 'intolerance' of the opinions, Mr White being most outspoken:

> We are a Catholic school. Statues and holy pictures are part of the Catholic way of life. They are in this school for the benefit of the people within the school, not for any outsiders who might visit us. If they take offence well that's too bad but it is also irrelevant. I think that it's typical of the general Protestant approach to Catholics – why should our religion offend them? I think they would prefer that we didn't exist at all.

Another teacher made a further point:

> All this talk about Catholic opposition to integration showing how intransigent we are is nonsense. Our schools exist because of a religious conviction, and not to cause offence to anyone. It's ridiculous to suggest that a picture of Our Lady was put up in order to offend Protestant visitors. Why can't Protestants understand and accept this? We don't want to give offence to anyone.

But might you not take them down if you knew they were causing offence?

Why the hell should we? These things are private and mean a lot to us; they are nothing to do with anyone else.

How much they meant, however, is a moot point. When I asked a group of teachers in St Judes to describe the religious emblem displayed in the entrance hall of the school, not one of them knew that there was one there or what it was!

The central point is that there seemed to be no intention to offend anyone by the display of rituals or symbols. It was simply unfortunate that they were perceived in this way by outsiders.

Here, then, is an important and often overlooked aspect of ritual. It may act as Bernstein (1971) and Skilbeck (1976) suggest, to bind people together as a distinctive collectivity or to preserve an identity. In a segregated society, however, served by segregated schools, it would seem that the more distinctive they are then the more suspicion and intolerance is engendered in outside observers who neither understand nor identify with the more overt signs which contribute to this distinctiveness. Whatever the intentions of the group, it would appear that distinctiveness is interpreted as exclusiveness and hence with suspicion.

Common Aspects of School Culture

The very many common curricular practices existing in both schools have already been referred to in this chapter. There was also an abundance of shared practices observed in both schools at a cultural level. These provided enough evidence to suggest the existance of a culture which was common to both schools. Farren (1976) has commented that this common cultural element in schools can be so powerful as to conceal any differences which may exist. This may be true if one adopts a quantitative or objective approach to culture in schools. However, a participant approach would suggest it to be an overstatement.

One aspect of the culture of schools might perhaps be described as 'leisure' or 'media' orientated since it exists predominantly at the level of sports or pastimes and the major influence in its fostering or reinforcement is television.

By its very nature the influence of the media tends to ensure that such a culture is both superficial and transitory in the sense that it is not direct human contact but rather a means of communication for a pluralistic audience. To be economically successful it must, therefore, strive for consensus rather than distinctiveness. This is not to suggest that television cannot be a major cultural influence but simply that, at the level of leisure or entertainment, its power of influence tends to be restricted and passive compared to the more atavistic and intense Protestant and Catholic cultures in Northern Ireland. Although Yeats could hardly have foreseen such an influence, it does perhaps represent a classic facilitator of 'the filthy western tide' which he claimed would eventually contaminate and destroy the endemic culture of Ireland.

Both schools, for example, were very involved in playing soccer and competed against each other, and all the other primary schools of the area, in the same league. Gaelic games are almost unknown in the area and so there is no conflict of choice for either teacher or pupils in the general arena of games for boys.

There were, in fact, as many Manchester United schoolbags apparent in St Judes as in Rathlin, and support for this and other English soccer teams was as intense in each school.

It is difficult to determine whether such unity transcends other cultural differences or can be sublimated within them. On one occasion pupils from Rathlin were fighting with those emerging from St Judes after school. This rare event was interesting in that opposing groups were demonstrating symbols which were common to them both – badges of particular pop stars or groups, soccer team schoolbags and scarfs and many presumably came from the same neighbourhoods. It was difficult to avoid the impression that one could easily shuffle the 'pack' and resume the altercation with totally different antagonists.

This underlying difference within a common activity was observed during a football match between St Judes and another state school from the area. One of the St Judes teachers was getting actively and vociferously involved in the action. I laughingly commented on his involvement and he retorted darkly, 'There is more to this than just football.' Although I felt that I knew what he meant I asked him later to elaborate on the statement. He was rather embarassed by what he saw as 'having to explain just a feeling'. He did expand, however, in stating that right throughout his school-days and even now as a teacher he had had the impression that Protestant schools were always more difficult to beat than Catholic ones. He knew this was ridiculous (St Judes was the best team in the league) but he claimed that it was another example of 'the old Catholic inferiority complex in Northern Ireland'. Van der Plas (1967) describes a similar perception which he observed with Dutch Catholics:

> There was a certain fear based on a social inferiority complex and a sense of not being a match for the 'better' Protestant.

A superficial approach to culture in schools can allow this common culture to obscure underlying differences. It is notable that although St Judes partook wholeheartedly in the common activity of football they were reluctant to lose their deeper identity within it. They wore a Glasgow Celtic strip for all home matches and for all away matches against Catholic schools, but changed to less evocative attire when playing away to Protestant schools. There was a perceived element of safety in the procedure, but the fact thay they retained the Celtic strip for 'safe' occasions is significant.

The normal interest of the young in 'pop' music seemed also common to both schools, as was its attendant culture. Even within this domain, however, there seemed to be subtle yet significant emphases. At the time of the deaths of Bing Crosby and Elvis Presley I heard one pupil in St Judes ask his teacher, 'Why did we pray for Bing Crosby but not for Elvis?' The teacher, in responding, gave the strong impression that in his eyes Crosby represented more of an establishment figure than his contemporary and as such warranted more respect. On the other hand, the former star has always been regarded as the epitome of 'a good Catholic' and as such was a member of a broad cultural group to which St Judes also belonged.

The stereotyped picture of a strict split between 'Catholic' sports like Gaelic football, hurling and camogie in Catholic schools and 'Protestant' sports like hockey, cricket and rugby in Protestant schools is far from accurate in the geographic area in which my research was carried out. It is true to say that these sports rarely cross the religious divide, but it is also important to state that they are practised in only a minority of primary schools. There is a third group of sports which were equally popular in Rathlin and St Judes – basketball, soccer and netball are examples. Other common activities within the schools were debating, singing festivals and swimming.

Although all of these activities represent common values and perhaps a common culture, they may paradoxically result in an accentuation of the differences between the schools. Murray (1980b) has demonstrated that joint cultural activites between Catholic and Protestant pupils can reinforce stereotypes by focussing the attention of participants on the differences between the groups.

This danger may be all the more likely when common activities take place in a competitive milieu, which was the case in the vast majority of contacts between Rathlin and St Judes. On one occasion I arrived at the school playing-fields as a young child was leaving. I asked how the match was going and was greeted with the despondent reply, 'Oh, the Protestants are winning 5-0'!

From observation within Rathlin and St Judes it would appear that, in the past, the beneficial effects of these shared activities have been overemphasised by commentators – especially since the bulk of them are competitive in nature. Impressions gained within the schools reinforced the view that they served more to emphasise differences between the two segregated systems than to increase sensitivity and tolerance within them.

This observation weakens the claim of the Roman Catholic hierarchy in Northern Ireland (Bishop C. Daly, 1978; Bishop E. Daly, 1980, 1981) that contact should be sought within the present segregated school system rather than striving for the 'pseudo-conformity' of an integrated system. While this view is understandable, it would seem that such contact will only prove beneficial in this respect if the competitive element is removed from it.

It is of interest that this more closely focussed study on two schools suggests that broader analyses, such as employed in the *Schools Apart* project, tend to conceal real differences in practice and experience. That report describes 'twinned schools', of which Rathlin and St Judes were examples, which had close administrative liaison, joint recreational activities and often unusually close relationships between principals. While it is true to say that many activities were common to both schools, there was little evidence to demonstrate the close relationships claimed by the *Schools Apart* authors. In fact, the bulk of joint activities could be argued to emphasise the differences, rather than to mould any special relationship, between them.

It is unfortunate that within the two schools such a gulf exists between intention and perception, since it is on the basis of both of these that social reality is constructed. At the level of ritual in the two schools, such realities would seem to be poles apart.

Nonetheless, it would be naive to suggest that in the Northern Ireland context symbols were never intended to be provocative. On the basis of observation and discussion in both schools, however, it seemed that perception of a provocative intent grossly exaggerated and misrepresented the intention itself. This may well also be true of society in general.

Skilbeck (1975) claims that it is very important to think of the images and symbols which communicate meanings and which structure behaviour. He argues that:

> The rituals carried out in an institution have certain meanings because of what that institution is trying to do.

One might have imagined, therefore, that since both schools studied were primary schools, operating in one area of a very small country, that the rituals within each would be rather similar. However, at the level of character and culture of the schools, this proved to be far from the case.

In fact, while it was observed that ritual tended to bind schools together in what Bernstein (1971) has referred to as a 'distinct collectivity', this was achieved on the basis of contrasting values, attitudes and meanings of individuals within the two schools. At a golbal level, therefore, ritual might be seen to emphasise distinctiveness rather than collectivity.

Distinctiveness is but a short step from divisiveness, and in this context it is argued that rituals and symbols existing within the segregated school system in Northern Ireland may well serve to perpetuate separateness and, because they seem so revered, ultimately prove to be major impediments to future attempts to integrate these school systems. Ritual and symbols in schools, therefore, should begin to be considered very seriously indeed.

4

Identity: A Covert
Pedagogy in Schools

I HAVE come to the conclusion over the years that treatments of the concept of 'identity' in Ireland, which have usually either been quarried from the misty slopes of the Boyne or illuminated by some celtic twilight, have continually yielded little to aid comprehension of identity in the Northern Ireland context. More can be learned about cultural realities in the province through a consideration of contemporary influences on identity. I am using the term here in terms of identity *with* rather than identity *of* individuals, groups and structures. It is to this aspect of identity that this chapter is addressed. Therefore, comment is made on the extent to which individuals and groups within the schools relate to (or identify with) government and state departments in Northern Ireland. It will be postulated that the disparity of response and observation in this context may be a major factor in explaining the curricular and cultural differences obtaining within the two schools, and indeed between the two segregated systems of education in general. Discussion of this latter claim is based, not only on my research within the two schools but also on my related work (Murray *et al.*, 1977; Murray 1979(a); Murray, 1979(b); Murray, 1980(a); Murray, 1980(b)).

This particular, and possibly idiosyncratic, definition of identity as being one aspect of culture is closely related to one's religion in Northern Ireland. It is, however, of more immediate relevance with regard to the civic and social behaviour of individuals and groups. At the specific level of the culture of the school, therefore, much can be learned by studying the extent to which members of St Jude's and Rathlin considered administration and policy-making bodies to be either natural and effective support systems, or merely meddlesome intruders.

It would seem remiss, therefore, that so little research has been carried out in Northern Ireland into how the two major cultural and religious groups perceive their identity. Even less has been carried out within schools. Robinson (1971), researching with school children in Derry schools, claims that Protestant children see themselves as living in Northern Ireland with their capital Belfast and their history as part of British history. Catholic children on the other hand see themselves as living in Ireland with Dublin as their capital and a history of their own.

If true, such findings are important in attempting to understand the civic behaviour of the two groups and as such are deserving of further, and deeper, consideration. Russell (1972), for example, has demonstrated that, arising out of this notion of identity, 'Catholics in Northern Ireland are more likely to display negative attitudes towards the (Northern Ireland) government'.

This specific conclusion of Russell's research relates very closely to my own definition of identity. I am convinced that more can be learned about it by a study of its contemporary ramifications than by blundering about in the mists and murk of previous centuries. This may seem gratuitous, but the stage has been reached in Northern Ireland where pragmatic (and contemporary) approaches are likely to be more productive than historic justification.

Since the concept of identity dealt with here is political in character, it should be seen in the context of prevailing political structures in Northern Ireland. In fact, the implementation of the state was carried out almost exclusively by Protestants. The Catholic population, being convinced that the system would never last, took little part in proceedings. They were content to await its imminent and inevitable demise. The fact that the state proved more durable than Catholics had anticipated had two main implications. In the first place, Catholics were badly represented at policy-making levels and secondly, and perhaps consequently, more concern was afforded to Protestant aspirations and values in the formation of legislation and admini-stration. This situation obtained as much in education as in other institutions.

While this power base was indisputably Protestant in nature, the existence of bias may have been exaggerated by Catholic perceptions. At the level of identity, however, whether gross bias existed in fact is less important than that it was seen to exist. It resulted in further avoidance by Catholics of existing political structures and reciprocal suspicion and exclusion of them by Protestants in government. Positive identity, on the one hand, and alienation and separatism, on the other hand, have become deep-rooted over the years.

This situation may well lend credence to the popular axiom (on the Catholics side at least) that antipathy towards them which is mooted by Protestants is usually couched in religious terms whereas any aversion articulated by Catholics against Protestants most often tends to concentrate on political aspirations.

This might be explained by the observation that overt political structures and institutions in Northern Ireland are equated by Catholics with the Protestant establishment and, as such, to be distrusted, or at least treated with caution. After all, it is these contemporary structures and institutions which epitomise everything which was abhorrent to Catholics at the time of the origin of the state of Northern Ireland. These, then, present graphic evidence (and perhaps 'legitimate targets') of the discordant aspirations held by Protestants.

Indeed, in St Jude's there was evidence to suggest that such negative attitudes were applied to structures which could hardly be seen as political. The impression was given that such institutions as the post office, the fire service, the life-boat service, etc. were also equated with a Protestant establishment.

For Protestants, on the other hand, there is a much more limited range of institutions in Northern Ireland which can be claimed to represent the political aspirations of Catholics. There are, of course, Catholic churches, Catholic schools and perhaps the Gaelic Athletic Association. All of these pre-date the state of Northern Ireland and as such are more likely to be seen by Protestants in an all-Ireland context. Obviously this has political implications. However, when Protestants look 'south' and observe what is for them the appalling influence which the Catholic church exerts over populace and politicians alike, it is little wonder that political and cultural considerations are seen as having less importance than the perceived religious hegemony of the Catholic church.

Thus, while reaction against Protestants from Catholics may most often be couched in political terms, Protestants may tend to posit religion as being the crucial and fundamental element of disparity.

Whatever the reasons for, or indeed the veracity of, this particular claim, it was considered essential in a cultural analysis of segregated schools in Northern Ireland to determine, firstly, if such varying perceptions of Church and State existed in schools and, secondly, to attempt to describe their practical implications for the day-to-day life and procedures of the schools.

In fact, very little work has been carried out in this area. Murray (1979a) attempted to show how such varying perceptions and attitudes can influence educational structures and to show how such varying perceptions and attitudes can influence educational structures and behaviour. He concludes with the general statement:

> It appeared that the Protestant schools identified almost totally with the administrative and policy making sections of the educational system (Department of Education, Education and Library Boards). These were deemed to be natural support structures, which through dissemination of information and close contact, moulded a solidarity among all state schools. There seemed to be a sense of belonging to, and identity with, a kind of extended educational family. Representatives from these bodies visited the school on open days and prize days and were known by, or at least recognisable to, teachers in state schools. Through communications from the department (sent only to state schools) teachers were kept aware of the current job situation – who had been promoted recently, where a vacancy had arisen, where 'so and so' is now, etc – all of which acted to mould state schools into a distinct and clearly identifiable group.
>
> Teachers in Catholic schools seemed to soldier on in a kind of parochial isolation in this respect. There was no such network of communication. Any information which did filter through was by word of mouth or through outside agencies such as newspapers. . . they were not only isolated from other Catholic schools but also from governmental support structures which seemed to form such an integral part of the state system.

This outline, in common with many other structural representations, is necessarily generalised in nature. It is useful perhaps in drawing attention to broad differences in outlook and procedures, but lacks precision by failing to demonstrate actual or specific differences in behaviour in schools attributable to varying perceptions of these structures. Close observation within Rathlin and St Judes provided much more specific information which can complement, and perhaps 'put meat on' the barer bones of this structural exposition.

During research in the two schools it became clear that in Rathlin there existed a positive attitude towards the Department of Education and the local Education and Library Board. They seemed to be seen as a natural extension of the school and an integral part of a system to which Rathlin itself belonged. In this sense there was a common group identity with good communication and relationships existing within the group. A brief extract from Mr Long's address at prize-giving demonstrates this feeling:

> We take for granted the support of the Library Boards whose staff are so helpful when we ask for their expert advice.

The fact that the chairman of the local Education and Library Board was present in the audience may will have had some influence on Mr Long's comments. His presence itself, however, demonstrates that he was considered to have an interest in and concern for the school. In fact, Mr Long served on several consultative committees with the chairman and knew him well.

The principal and staff in St Judes appeared to view educational legislative bodies as 'outsiders'; necessities to be tolerated. On one occasion Mr Matthews entered the staffroom at break-time brandishing a letter from the Department of Education. It was about some quite trivial matter but he used it to demonstrate the bureaucracy of the system. He went on at great length about the interference by the department in the running of the school. The whole tenor of his remarks suggested anything but a mutual concern for the education of the pupils.

This perceived intrusiveness permeated all discussions and actions of individuals in St Judes. One morning a stranger was observed passing the staffroom window. It transpired that he was an employee of the Education and Library Board who was servicing the heating system of the school. As soon as this fact was established the resentment in the room became almost tangible – 'I wonder what he gets paid?' and 'Whatever it is it is too much' were typical comments. I asked the group closest to me if they would prefer to be without heating. One replied that it was just a case of not liking *them* to be 'poking about'. This particular pronoun was often used pejoratively to describe educational officialdom.

During an interview with another Catholic principal in the area I was informed that when a window was broken, he always insisted that the culprit pay for the damage. There were two reasons for this. In the first place it was good training for the pupils as they learned a a sense of responsibility. Secondly:

> It saves me having to get in touch with the board and have *them* crawling all over the place.

This attitude contrasts starkly with that of Mr Long in Rathlin. He was obviously proud (and frequently discussed) his record of getting things done by the board. According to the secretary in the school he was 'never off the phone to one body or another'.

These particular attitudes may well be symptomatic of a general trend. One senior Library Board official informed me that his office received ten times as many enquiries of a banal nature from state schools as from Catholic schools. Although this could scarcely be seen as hard statistical evidence it does nonetheless provide further evidence to support the more interpretive data suggesting that Catholic schools are less inclined to perceive official bodies as being natural support systems for their schools.

This can be taken a stage further. Not only may the Catholic school not perceive officials of administration as colleagues with a common goal, but they may be seen as 'the opposition'. Examples which suggest this possibility were recorded in three different Catholic primary schools in the area.

In one such school the principal informed me that he had applied to the department to close the school for a day because of the death of a past teacher. The department refused but the school quietly closed anyway – 'What right had they to tell us what to do?'

In another school, during the oil shortage, a general ban was placed on after-school activities. The principal still arranged a parent/teacher meeting on a particular night. He stated:

> But I'll be damned if I'll tell the board. My management committee have said its O.K. and that is good enough for me.

In St Judes, Mr Matthews told me that the school always gave free school meals to all visitors (visiting teachers, teaching supervisors, etc.) although officially he was not supposed to do this. In fact, I checked with several such supervisors and all that I spoke to agreed that they were more likely to be offered a free meal in a Catholic school than in a state school. This again demonstrates an identification disparity between the two groups. In state schools any irregularities within the educational system are carried out against themselves since they perceive themselves as part of that system. Catholic schools labour under no such constraints and hence may find such 'generosity' easier to practise.

In fact, Mr Matthews told me that there were several pupils in his school who did not qualify for free school dinners but they got them just the same. He contended that 'you will not see this happening in Rathlin'. He seemed to actually take pride in this kind of 'fiddling' of the system when it was for the benefit of his pupils. His rationale seemed to be a good example of the general Catholic claim (Furton 1973) that the child is a child first and only secondly a citizen. There was no possibility of misreading the *them* (government bodies) and *us* (Catholic schools) imputation in his remarks and actions.

This kind of negative relationship was not confined to educational bodies. I commented to the staff in St Judes that in Rathlin the children went on more trips to the fire station, local government offices, the post office, the police station, etc. They all agreed that this was probably so but argued that it would be a waste of time for them to do so since 'our kids will never get a job in any of them' (because they were Catholics).

It was interesting that the staff saw such outings in occupational terms only. They also considered such establishments as bastions of exclusive Protestant employment, which numerically is far from true. What is more disconcerting is that such negative perceptions within the school may well curtail the occupational aspirations and possibilities of the pupils. They may well not apply to these work sources because of the axiomatic knowledge, derived from teachers. Thus, not only are the expectations of pupils being affected but their aspirations are also being curtailed.

It is also possible that the positive attitudes towards government bodies experienced in state schools may affect curricular practice. The experience of the *Schools Cultural Studies Project* (1981) provides a case in point. Briefly, this project attempted to have pupils clarify cultural and social values rather than accept either set as being axiomatic. It adopted a relativistic rather than absolutist approach to culture in Northern Ireland. The project had much more success in Catholic schools than in state schools, with three times as many of the former adopting it as the latter.

From interviews with teachers in schools which had either accepted or rejected the project, Murray (1979a) claims:

> Any attempt to introduce an innovation which requires participants to question hitherto sacrosanct societal values will be likely to evoke different responses from the two existing educational systems. On the one hand, Catholic schools, which may have had no great empathy with such norms, may find it expedient to embrace such an innovation. On the other, staffs in state schools may see any such assault on the *status quo* as a positive threat to their position and as such to be opposed, or at least, ignored.

It would seem, therefore, that the perceptions of identity of teachers can influence the educational experiences of their pupils.

These disparate identifications might also be understood in other than historical terms. It could be that Catholic schools experience more schizophrenia with regard to their perceptions of an educational power base than do state schools. It appeared that in St Judes the Department of Education and the Education and Library Boards were attributed with a more restricted role than was the case in Rathlin. Restricted, that is, as much as possible to an administrative function.

While the 'eleven plus' examination exerted a common central constraint on both schools, the teachers in St Judes contended that what went on outside this was a matter for themselves as Catholics. The church, and the fact that the school was Catholic, were seen to be the major determinants of school policy and practice.

More specifically, within the sphere of education claimed to be most important by Catholics (i.e. moral development), state bodies were attributed with minimal concern. This may prove to be of fundamental importance in accounting for philosophical, perceptual and practical differences between the Catholic system and the state system of education in Northern Ireland.

The relative identification of schools with the church would appear to be of crucial importance in understanding differences in attitudes and practice between the two systems. It is essential, therefore, to describe and comment upon specific manifestations of it observed within St Judes and Rathlin.

At the outset, it should be stated that the rather patronising tendency of Catholics to refer to all others of different faiths as 'non-Catholics', does little to illuminate the variety of creeds within Rathlin. Although Protestant in composition, it was by no means homogenously so. (*see* Table 4:1). This diversity of beliefs and interests is an important factor in any comparison of relative church influence and identity in Catholic and Protestant schools.

Table 4:1

RELIGIOUS DENOMINATIONS OF CHILDREN
ATTENDING RATHLIN SCHOOL

Class	No.	Boys	Girls	C. of I.	Pres.	Meth.	R/C	Others
P1/2	30	10	20	8	17	—	1	4
1E	32	20	12	12	15	—	—	4
1J	31	20	11	8	14	—	—	9
2I	27	13	14	4	16	—	—	7
P2D	27	10	17	11	11	2	—	3
P3B	34	21	13	13	15	1	—	5
3C	34	14	20	16	15	—	—	3
P4McC	35	21	14	2	17	—	1	15
4J	35	19	16	10	17	2	1	5
5/6C	35	16	19	9	20	1	—	5
5B	35	18	17	14	15	1	2	3
P6	35	15	20	16	15	2	—	3
P7W	32	14	18	11	16	2	1	4
P7M	32	15	17	12	12	—	1	7
	454	226	228	146	215	10	6	77

On the other hand, since Catholic schools proclaim their catholicity and, in fact, insist on remaining so, this must increase the influence of that particular church within them.

At first sight, therefore, it was surprising that the visible presence of clergy in the schools was much more marked in Rathlin than St Judes. In the former school, three ministers attended assembly every Tuesday and also took religious classes on that day from 9.00 a.m until 9.30. They also attended most of the public functions in the school (prize days, pageants, carol services, etc.). All were personally known to the staff and their presence was considered natural and unremarkable.

In St Judes, on the other hand, I only saw the parish priest once during the whole period of observation. Several teachers told me that the only time they had talked to him was at interview for their appointment. One told me, 'In the seven years I have been here the priest has not been in my classroom once.' Another claimed, 'You could never tell that this was a Catholic school from the number of visits we get from our priests.' And again, 'This business about the close links betwen the Catholic school and the Catholic church is a load of bull – we just never see them.'

It would be a mistake, however, to equate church influence with overt presence. In the Catholic school it became apparent that church authority only became evident when circumstances demanded it. It should be remembered that principal and vice principal (and indeed all of the staff) had been appointed by a management committee, on which church representatives had a majority vote. It is not unreasonable to assume that selection is made on the basis of how well candidates will function in a Catholic school – ('I would not have got this job if I had not been a parishioner'). If, therefore, this selection process is 'successful' then direct clerical intervention becomes superfluous thereafter. This system, however, proved not to be infallible in St Judes.

Several years after the appointment of one male member of staff, it was discovered that he had married a Protestant. The parish priest immediately asked him to resign. The teacher told me that he was informed that he could no longer teach in a Catholic school with his history; it would be a bad example for the pupils in the school. He refused to resign and took his case, significantly, to the Catholic teachers union, the Irish National Teachers Organisation, rather than to the Department of Education. After a long 'wrangle' he won his case and now continues to teach in St Judes.

Another event demonstrated greater success for the church authorities. During the year of my observation in St Judes a new teacher was appointed. Some time later it was discovered by the staff that he was not fully qualified and was required by the Department of Education to repeat his final year at teacher training college. The parish priest insisted that the resulting vacancy should be advertised as a one-year appointment only. The staff were enraged because one of their number was being made redundant at the same time. They claimed that she should get the job and tenure. They explained to me that the person who was unqualified was a parishioner and 'a paragon of the church' while the qualified teacher, who was losing her job, was not. I checked with some members of the staff the following year and they informed me that, in fact, the post was offered for one year only and filled for that one year by the hitherto mentioned qualified teacher. (At the end of the year, the unqualified teacher returned and is now working permanently in the school.)

Although these phenomena do nothing more than suggest that the church authorities retain a conviction of a right, or duty, to intervene in internal school affairs, there were other examples which implied that individuals within St Judes were both well aware of their limited autonomy and prepared to comply with it.

The secretary of the school informed me that at her interview the parish priest had commented that he had noticed that she did not attend mass in his church although she lived in the parish. He then asked her directly where she did go to mass. She explained that she went to a neighbouring parish because the times of masses were more convenient for her. This presumably was a satisfactory answer, since she got the job! The point is that she considered the question to be perfectly natural in an interview for a clerical post.

I was told by Mr Matthews that on one occasion a member of his staff was ill and the only substitute teacher he could find happened to be a Protestant. Although the period requiring cover was only two days, Mr Matthews still felt that he 'had to clear it with the parish priest first'. He stated that he would have experienced no such constraint had the potential substitute been a Catholic.

There seemed to be discrete, distinct and tacitly accepted domains of school life within which power was conceded to the church authorities. These were unwritten but nonetheless clearly understood. In the light of this mutual acknowledgement, the low visibility of clergy in St Judes becomes less surprising. There is in fact no necessity for a high profile if the areas of respective responsibility between church and school are clearly understood. This, of course, begs the question of how such a system of mutual comprehension of unwritten laws is perpetuated.

Perhaps the answer to this general question is highlighted by the specific example of the job of the unqualified teacher being safeguarded by the parish priest despite opposition from staff. The teachers in St Judes saw this simply in terms of him being a parishioner. This indeed may well have been so, but the implications of such an assertion require study in more detail.

In this context there is more of a tradition in state schools of 'outside' appointments being made to the schools. This may be because each school within the state system is also part of a much larger system. Every member of that system considers it natural and realistic to apply for a position anywhere within that system. As already mentioned, information about vacancies in state schools everywhere in Northern Ireland is circulated monthly to all state schools. No such internal communication organ exists in maintained schools. Each Catholic school tends to be identified firstly with its parish, secondly with the church as a whole and thirdly, and in the arena of appointments, almost peripherally with the state authorities.

Applicants who are known, and whose families are known, personally to management committees in Catholic schools will obviously have an advantage. This will almost inevitably result in people who are from the parish in which the school is situated being appointed. Since there is a greater history in Catholic schools of appointing vice-principals and principals from within the schools, young aspirants can expect eventually to get promotion within their original parish school.

(In St Judes both Ms Elder and Mr Matthews were appointed to their positions after twenty-five years service in the school. In Rathlin both Mr Long and Mr McCurdy were appointed from other schools.)

The operation of this process must act to preserve the parochiality of the Catholic school. More important, however, is that such a prolonged and persistent apprenticeship will provide an ideal milieu in which the ground rules of relative church and school responsibility can be learned. The subsequent (internal) appointments to vice-principal and principal can almost be assumed by clergy to subscribe to a tried and tested system of relative control. Thus, any need for frequent incursions into the school by clergy is obviated. It must be emphasised that St Judes may not be typical in this respect. Obviously some priests will view their pastoral responsibilities in a different light from others. Some may feel it incumbent upon themselves to visit their schools more frequently than was the case in St Judes.

It is also worthy of note that when the question of schools *vis-à-vis* external agencies was discussed with both staffs, it seemed always to be perceived exclusively in terms of the relative freedom of Catholic schools. It is likely that state schools, which are built, maintained and administered by area boards, will in fact differ in degree of autonomy from maintained schools. Indeed, several of the staff in Rathlin complained that maintained schools got all the 'perks' and did not have to account for them. While this stereotype is far from true, it demonstrates that autonomy was seen in terms of freedom from state intervention only. Even the staff in St Judes emphasised this particular aspect of autonomy, although on other occasions they seemed resentful of the power of the church in their school.

It would seem, therefore, that while both schools valued the ability to operate freely, each relinquished an element of such freedom to external bodies – Rathlin more to area boards and St Judes to the church authorities. This was on the whole willingly done, since these external agencies were identified as natural and apposite bodies who should have a legitimate concern for the functioning of the schools. Since these external bodies themselves have concern for different aspects of education in general, the relative identification of schools with them can be argued to be a major factor affecting rationale and behaviour in such schools.

In the context of relative identification with state institutions in Northern Ireland, the attitudes and behaviour observed in St Judes and Rathlin seemed to reflect those which are claimed to exist in society as a whole. In fact, the difference in the degree of identification of the schools with state and church bodies is argued to constitute one of the biggest differences between Rathlin and St Judes. In the former, there existed a positive attitude towards the local Education and Library Board, while the staff in St Judes seemed to see such bodies as outsiders which had, at best, to be tolerated. This is not to suggest that there was some kind of 'love affair' between Rathlin and institutional authority. However, the individuals within each met regularly and seemed to be striving towards a common goal.

In contrast, the staff in St Judes appeared to perceive institutional interest in terms of unwarranted, and unwanted, interference and in some cases actually strove to thwart it. It is possible that in certain circumstances this antipathy may restrict the vocational opportunities of pupils by predisposing them against jobs in what is seen as the establishment sector.

Within the sphere of moral development, state bodies were attributed with minimal authority by St Judes staff. Since this is the central concern of all Catholic schools, this fact is held to be of fundamental importance in distinguishing between the Catholic and state systems of education in Northern Ireland.

5

Stereotypes:
Invective and Invention

ONE of the central objectives of this study was to investigate the commonly held belief that there is a real difference in the experiences undergone by Catholic and Protestant children within their denominational schools in Northern Ireland. The intention was therefore to provide information which might enable the claim to be more rationally defended or rejected. An attempt has already been made in this respect in Chapters 3 and 4 where similarities and differences are described under the headings of culture and identity. This chapter tries to illuminate the ways in which the two school groups viewed each other in the light of the real, or imagined differences. This is attempted through a consideration of the stereotypes voiced by participants.

It must be said at once that stereotypes are general statements or perceptions of other groups which can be differentiated on an ethnic, national, or religious basis. (It would not be possible, for example, to hold a stereotype about someone whom we know well since in this case we would have enough information at hand to enable us to treat that person as an individual.)

It might be argued, therefore, that a study of only two schools cannot provide enough generalised information to test the veracity of such general statements. My goal was not to generalise, but rather to record and analyse stereotypes which were articulated by the participants to demonstrate their views about other individuals and groups. I was in an enviable and unique position to do this since I had a personal knowledge and experience of both the individuals who were voicing the stereotypes and also the contexts towards which they were being applied. Many of the stereotypes which were recorded in Rathlin, for example, were directed towards the other researched group, i.e. St Judes. This was partly due to my influence. It was also inevitable, since the Rathlin teachers were well aware that I was also researching in St

Judes.

This has important implications, since stereotypes were being voiced (in total and self-confessed ignorance) by both Rathlin and St Judes teachers about groups and institutions with and within which I had researched. Thus, to some extent at least, I was able to ground these ill-informed stereotypes in a personal awareness of the individuals against whom they were directed.

Unfortunately, there has been up until now a high level of mutual ignorance about the two sets of schools. This ignorance is perpetuated, and perhaps exaggerated, by the fact that it is relatively rare for Protestant teachers to teach in Catholic schools and vice versa. Virtually nothing is known at first hand about the day-to-day running of the other school system. Judgements and descriptions have, therefore, tended to be articulated at an axiomatic or stereotypical level. This is in itself undesirable. Of even more concern is the evidence (Darby *et al.*, 1977; Murray, 1978) that there is also a degree of mutual suspicion arising, at least in part, from this ignorance. It would seem that if the debate on segregated education continues to be carried on at this stereotypical level, there will be little opportunity for increased awareness or understanding, especially among teachers.

It was considered essential, therefore, to give consideration to perceptions (or stereotypes) of the teachers in both St Judes and Rathlin in the light of my observation within these establishments. As will be discussed later, it is these (mainly unfavourable) stereotypes which present major obstacles to increased contact between the two school systems, not to mention integration of them. This possibility is demonstrated by Ehrlich's (1976) view of stereotypes:

> Stereotypes, as the language of prejudice, are thought to provide a vocabulary of motives both for individuals and the concerted action of prejudiced persons. They signal the socially approved and accessible targets for the release of hostility and aggression and they provide the rationalisations for prejudiced attitudes and discriminatory behaviour.

The crucial point here, in the context of Northern Irish schools, is that stereotypes of teachers may serve to maintain solidarity and hence perpetuate separateness. They are, therefore, worthy of very serious consideration.

Information about the perceptions of both groups was gathered in general conversation – 'Jeepers! We shouldn't be talking like this with you here. . .'– and at interview, where respondants gave careful consideration to my questions. The consistency of stated attitudes within each group was remarkable. They are treated here under three main headings: stereotypes held by Protestant teachers; stereotypes held by Catholic teachers; the children's stereotypes.

However, since the stereotypes are grounded in observation of the actual contexts within and about which they were being articulated, there will inevitably be considerable overlap in their presentation.

Stereotypes held by Protestant Teachers

The most commonly expressed view about Catholic schools in general, and St Judes in particular, was that they were 'priest-ridden'. It was impressive how often this actual phrase was used by Rathlin teachers. It seemed as if it were accepted as a definition of Catholic schools and this 'fact' was held to affect significantly the atmosphere and behaviour within them.

This notion was summed up by Ms Barnes:

> You see it has all got to do with expectations. The priests expect women to have plenty of children. I would hate to teach in St Judes because I have only two (children). I think, therefore, I would feel threatened.

I pointed out that Ms Elder, the vice-principal in St Judes, had no children, to which Ms Barnes repled, 'Oh I'm sure there are exceptions, but I'm talking in general terms.'

This would seem demonstrate that, in the context of stereotypes, hearsay is more important than actual evidence. It is also important to restate that all the teachers expressed a total ignorance of what went on in 'the other type of school'.

Ms Jackson commented on the influence of the church on Catholic schools. In reference to another primary school in the town she told me:

> Whenever I go there I always get the impression that the lay staff are terrified of the nuns. (Laughing) I certainly am. Also the priests are in all the time. The staff, therefore, cannot express themselves. I am convinced that teachers in state schools have far more freedom.

In connection with Ms Jackson's central concern, I made a point of publicly stating to the whole staff in Rathlin that during my time spent in St Judes I had only seen the priest once in the school. I also emphasised that ministers were in Rathlin every week. The staff reaction was universal. They seemed genuinely surprised and not a little sceptical about the low profile of priests in St Judes.

Their reaction to my second point about ministers in Rathlin was rather more interesting. Many of them claimed that there was no comparison between the two examples because 'here the ministers only come in for a half an hour or so and only do what they are supposed to do'. The strong implication was that priests in St Judes and other Catholic schools overstepped this mark. The Rathlin staff seemed to have very clear views on the extent to which ministers should be involved in schools and authority which they should have there. They saw the level of authority of priests in the Catholic sector in terms of gross excess. This is obviously related to the acceptance of the authority of clergy by Protestants and Catholics in general.

In this context, the more overtly signs of the catholicity of Catholic schools are displayed, the more unappealing they become to Protestant teachers. Ms Walker gave a flavour of this aversion:

> I heard a priest once arguing for the all-pervasive nature of religion in Catholic schools. I remember thinking that their schools must be grim.

This lack of empathy was not restricted to religious matters. Many of the Rathlin teachers interviewed claimed that the curriculum would be different in St Judes. The point was made by Mr Smyth:

> I think that their [St Judes] teaching of history would be impassioned and biased. Here we teach it as it is.

There was also a general feeling that there would be more singing and dancing in St Judes. In fact, this was quite mistaken. Much more of this kind of activity was observed in Rathlin.

There was also a conviction, mooted in the majority of interviews, that Catholic teachers make positive efforts to inculcate the nationalist culture in their pupils. I asked many of the Rathlin teachers if they considered that they, or the school, encouraged a British culture. Strangely, not one of them did. Perhaps this was because, just as in St

Judes, it had become so natural as to be unconscious.
Catholic teachers in general were seen as more ambitious and 'pushy'.
'Proof' of this was demonstrated daily. Ms Kyle (remedial teacher)
claimed:

> No matter what course I attend there is always a majority of
> Catholics there – and nine times out of ten the course is actually
> being given by a Catholic.

A principal from another state school in the area whom I interviewed
(and who thought I was a Protestant) explained how this was achieved:

> In Catholic schools, the moment literature comes in about a course,
> it is shown to all the staff. There is a general rush to fill it in and
> apply. It is always posted back the same day. The result is that there
> is no room on the course for the (more tardy) Protestants.

The reason given for this Catholic single-mindedness was that they
perceived themselves to be, or have been, discriminated against and
this drove them to get better qualifications in order to 'get ahead'.

Catholics in public life were also seen to be better prepared (a direct
contradiction of the Catholic stereotype). Ms Creighton explained:

> It always infuriates me that if there is a debate on television about
> politics or whatever, it always seems to be between an eloquent
> Catholic and an inarticulate blustering Protestant. I invariably feel
> let down.

In general the behaviour of Catholic teachers was seen to be less
responsible than that of Protestants. This was perhaps the most general
attitude experienced both in general conversation and at interview. It
seemed that Catholic behaviour offended some kind of Protestant ethic
of propriety. Early on in the interviewing stage of the research in Rathlin
several teachers contended that there would be less manners taught in
St Judes – 'We emphasise that here'. Subsequently, I asked a specific
question on this aspect of behaviour. It transpired that every member
of Rathlin staff held this view. Ms Creighton claimed that the teachers
themselves are less well-mannered and:

> Catholic female teachers curse much more than we do. They also
> tend to be more untidy.

This absence of 'proper' behaviour was demonstrated often to Rathlin teachers. On one occasion Ms Murray was attempting to arrange a basketball match with St Judes. She returned to the staffroom after telephoning, to recount the experience. She explained, almost incredulously, that when she asked the teacher in St Judes when they would be willing to play, the reply was, 'Oh, anytime you want'. Ms Murray exclaimed:

> They would have played at ten o'clock in the morning if I had suggested it!

This was greeted with chortles and knowing looks from the assembled staff. It seemed (and was later confirmed in conversation) that the teachers regarded this kind of cavalier attitude to schooling as a uniquely Catholic one. To play games during school time just wasn't proper or responsible behaviour for teachers to encourage.

At this same session, as a result of Ms Murray's comments, I recounted some of my observations in St Judes which I considered relevant. At Christmas the teachers there had their seasonal lunch in the dinner hall with the children. Several bottles of wine, supplied by Mr Matthews, were consumed at the meal. The behaviour of the teachers was loud and boisterous.

On another occasion, during a wet lunch hour, the staff presented a knock-out table tennis competition on the stage of the assembly hall. Everyone took part, from Mr Matthews to myself. There was much horseplay and play-acting which was hugely enjoyed by the children.

The reaction of the Rathlin staff to these anecdotes was uniform. This was especially so with reference to the public demonstration of wine drinking. Ms Walker voiced the general view:

> You see, that is exactly what I mean. I have worked in several (state) schools and this is the most informal that I have been in. But still you would never get that sort of thing happening here.

It must be appreciated, however, that this behaviour in St Judes may have been determined, or at least facilitated, by the *character* of the institution. This, however, is largely irrelevant. The Rathlin staff perceived it in the context of the participants being Catholic, i.e. very much in *cultural* terms. The behaviour, therefore, was seen to reinforce their previously held views on general behaviour in Catholic schools.

The example of the public table tennis match stimulated a general conversation among the Rathlin staff present on the relative relationships between Catholic and Protestant teachers and their pupils. In fact, this concept seemed to provide a fundamental difference in perception and observation between the two schools.

In St Judes, teachers were continually laughing and joking with the children. Many teachers, on meeting children in the corridor, would playfully punch or wrestle with them or dramatically threaten them. This was always taken in good spirit by all involved. Also the children were constantly referred to as 'darling', 'dear' or 'love'. This kind of rapport was rarely observed in Rathlin. I discussed these differences with Mr Long and he replied, 'You're right, I don't think I could have that.'

The atmosphere in Rathlin came closest to the normal of St Judes during the days of the annual pageant. The school reeked with barely controlled excitement. Children were involved constantly in animated conversation with their teachers about cues, lines, positions on stage, etc. The normal distancing of teacher and pupil seemed to be significantly eroded. I had not observed such camaraderie before. On at least three occasions, however, Mr Long seemed to feel compelled to justify it all to me:

> We'll soon be back to normal work; there's a strong historical element in the pageant [i.e. it was not a waste of time]; we'll all have settled down on Monday.

In fact he was quite right. By Monday the normal, and what seemed to me formal, relationships between teacher and pupil had returned. I was impressed with this rapid transformation and mentioned it to several teachers. They all agreed that for the school to work properly, you could not get 'too familiar' with the pupils. I mentioned the normal relationships in St Judes and they agreed that this was not surprising. Ms Barnes explained why:

> In general Catholics care more for the children. This is probably because they have larger families. I'm not surprised that there is more of a family atmosphere in their schools.

Surprisingly, the four teachers who were present all agreed. This 'more caring' stereotype was mentioned by seven teachers at interview later and was one of the very few favourable attitudes expressed. However, this attitude can only be seen as favourable if 'a family atmosphere' is construed as a compliment. In the context of school, it may not have been intended as such by the Rathlin teachers.

Finally, comments from two teachers demonstrated the pernicious potential of stereotypes, but also that they need not be immutable. Ms Thompson, a teacher from England, confided in me:

> I have heard them talking here that Catholics have different skin or different eyes. I know this is ridiculous, but now I find myself looking at people and wondering.

and Ms Creighton:

> I have recently moved house to an area in which there are a lot of Catholics. I'm only just realising how decent they are. . .

Stereotypes held by Catholic Teachers

Although physically the distance between St Judes and Rathlin is only 300 metres, the attitudinal chasm which existed between the teachers within them seemed hardly to reflect this geographical proximity.

Skilbeck (1976) described the two cultural communities in Northern Ireland existing in a kind of 'paradoxical symbiosis; complimentary entities sustained by tribal myths and mutual stereotyping'. This was clearly demonstrated by the two groups of teachers.

As in Rathlin, the consistency of expression of stereotypes by the teachers in St Judes was truly impressive. As the time approached for me to leave St Judes and go to Rathlin, the teachers in the former became more aware of the comparative element of the research. They seemed to realise that not only had they been observed as a group but also that they were going to be compared with another group of teachers from a state (Protestant) school. This realisation seemed to engender a kind of self-conciousness among the St Judes staff. This was demonstrated by almost constant expressions of advice (and sympathy) for me on my imminent experience:

> They'll be talking about theory and the curriculum all the time down there; you'll have no crack at all; I bet you'll not be allowed to smoke either; their staffroom will be dead tidy – you'll not enjoy yourself at all.

These were all comments to me which reflected the general feeling about my impending departure. There was also a strong implied sense of inferiority that 'the Protestants will show us up'. This was demonstrated by many comments and also by an experience which occurred on my second day in Rathlin.

As I was leaving the school at four o'clock, I was startled by the screeching of brakes. Two cars filled with teachers from St Judes had stopped and I was bundled unceremoniously into one of them, which then drove on for several hundred yards (out of sight of Rathlin). Both cars then stopped and all of the teachers gathered around the one I was in. I was 'grilled' for thirty minutes about how well St Judes was standing up to comparison!

I realised that this concern may have been apparent in any comparison, but two points are important. In the first place, the St Judes staff *assumed* that Rathlin would appear 'better'. Secondly, in all my time in Rathlin not one teacher expressed any kind of anxiety about the comparative element of research. In fact even when it was mentioned they seemed quite unconcerned.

This sense of inferiority seemed to be based largely on a general conviction that it was the nature of Protestants to be, at least publicly, better organised. Arising out of general staffroom conversation on this point, Mr White claimed:

> All you have to do is go to any teachers' meeting and you can pick out the Protestants a mile away. They are the ones who take their places early, are well scrubbed and have files and pens ready to take notes. The Catholics will always be found in a group outside the door having a last drag at a cigarette and looking for envelopes and scraps of paper to write on.

This in no way should be interpreted as a compliment to Protestant teachers. What was continually emphasised by the St Judes staff was that this was only a public image (i.e. the one that would impress) and that little lay behind it. As Mr White elaborated:

> You see we (Catholic teachers) don't have to put up a show. They (Protestant teachers) only go to these meetings to get ideas rather than to give them. They teach to a laid down pattern and hence are more staid and accepting. They are never taught to question and so they always conform. I am convinced that generally Protestants are less imaginative than Catholics.

What Protestant teachers were seen to lack in imagination was held to be recompensed to some degree by their conscientiousness. It was generally thought that they would work harder, be better prepared and be less likely to 'duck responsibility'.

Ms Eakin remembered me telling her that the staff in Rathlin had complained at having to take off class time in order to check that the pupils slippers and blazers had been labelled properly. This had obviously impressed her (as well as reinforcing her stereotype of the conscientious Protestant). She recounted the story to the assembled staff. They took this as vindication of their views – 'we would have jumped at the chance'.

On another occasion the point was made that across the spectrum of social action, Protestants were more law-abiding than Catholics. This was seen in terms of their differing identification with the state of Northern Ireland itself. For example, Mr White explained, Protestants always taxed their cars and would report misdemeanours to the police. Catholics would certainly be loathe to do the latter. He also claimed that 'Moore would not get a free dinner in Rathlin' (a reference to a pupil who did not qualify for free dinners but received them anyway for charitable reasons). The concept of identity has been discussed more fully in Chapter 4. Suffice to restate here that all the staff in St Judes saw the differing relations with institutional power as a major factor in distinguishing the perceptions and behaviour of Catholics and Protestants in Northern Ireland.

It was seen to explain, in part at least, what St Judes saw as conformity and staidness in the Protestant personality (two of the most common descriptions), and Mr Murphy enlarged on this point:

> You see, they are obsessed with doing the right thing, conforming all the time. They don't get drunk or tell dirty jokes or let their hair down simply because they are afraid of what people will say. They can't help being narrow-minded and humourless. This must affect the teaching in Protestant schools because if you haven't a sense of humour, you shouldn't be teaching. But I suppose it's just the Presbyterian way.

It seemed that Protestant teachers must not only continue to 'do the right thing' but also be *seen* to be doing it. During an interview Mr Jenkins told me:

They are so obsessed with their public image that they feel they have to be continually in the public eye. That's why they have more open days, prize days and publicity than we do.

In fact, Rathlin did engage in these types of activity much more frequently than did St Judes. This fact was not lost on the staff within the latter! It was interesting that just as any demonstration of the catholicity of St Judes was perceived by Rathlin staff to compound their stereotypes, the same applied to St Judes teachers with regard to the publicity emanating from Rathlin.

It is difficult to over-emphasise that, extreme as these views may appear, they were consistently (indeed unanimously) held by the St Judes teachers. Unfortunately they formed the basis for comparisons not only between St Judes and Rathlin but also between Catholic and Protestant schools in general.

All the staff were asked at interview how they thought that Rathlin would differ from their own school. They all responded within a very narrow range of adjectives – cold, rigid humourless, staid, un-imaginative, narrow-minded and (incredibly), bigots. I actively sought to elicit a favourable stereotype but did not succeed. Protestant teachers were in fact generally seen to be more 'hardworking', but even this was perceived in terms of conformity or a drive to do the right thing.

On one occasion I mentioned that I had found many of the staff in Rathlin to be both friendly and 'good crack'. Just as in Rathlin, however, such an input from me was greeted with either scepticism or cynicism. Ms Eakin demonstrated both:

> Of course there may well be exceptions but I wouldn't be surprised if they acted that way simply because you (presumably as a Catholic) were there.

This rigidity was seen to be the major difference between the two systems of schooling. The general argument was that children were all important. The St Judes teachers thought that they could show their emotions more than Protestant teachers and hence better demonstrate their love for children. Thus it was claimed that they were in fact better than state schools 'where it really counts'.

It is interesting that the public debate on integration of schools in Northern Ireland usually centers around the relative merit or defensibility of *Catholic* education. The teachers at St Judes, however, rarely mentioned this aspect of their school and certainly never claimed it as an advantage. They seemed rather to base their defence (if such it was) on the relative short-comings of the state schools.

Indeed comments made by staff in St Judes about church and clergy were almost always derogatory. They seemed offended by the dishonesty of the Catholic church in extolling the the trinity of church/family/school combining to educate the young. In their view no such trinity existed – 'it's all a load of bull'. If this is the case, and in St Judes in certainly seemed to be, then it is ironic that the greatest publicly acclaimed factor for the continuance of segregated schools may in many cases not exist.

The Children's Stereotypes

The observation and recording of the stereotypes held by the pupils of St Judes and Rathlin was curtailed by the expressed wish of both principals that I should not discuss sensitive issues with the children. Neither had any objection, however, to me asking the pupils to write an essay on 'How my School Compares With the One Nearest It'. This title included both the researched schools.

Both P6 and P7 classes in each school completed the essays and in all 108 were collected. It transpired that many of these were of less use than had been anticipated. The majority consisted of either eulogies or tirades about the child's own school. While these contributed useful information for other aspects of this research, they presented little information about the stereotypes held by children of a school enviroment about which they did not have first-hand knowledge.

The remainder did, however, provide some useful data. Every child who wrote an essay was aware of the religious differences between the two schools i.e. that one was Catholic and the other Protestant. While this was merely mentioned in many essays, those who elaborated demonstrated a rather suprising trend. In direct contrast to their teachers, the Protestant children articulated the differences in terms of pupil and teacher behaviour while the Catholic pupils saw the differences solely in religious terms. One depressing trait which they all shared with their teachers was that positive stereotypes were conspicuous by their absence.

Some of the attitudes expressed were common to both groups: 'You get a better education here', 'our teachers are better than theirs', etc. As I have said, however, the Catholic children tended to emphasise the religious aspect of schooling. They were well aware of why they were attending St Judes – 'my mother sent me here because I am a Catholic' – and also had a vague idea that their needs would not be met in Rathlin:

> The teachers there [Rathlin] don't say prayers. If I went there I would have to pray before I got there in the morning. Here we say prayers and sing hymns during the day.

> We learn about first holy communion here, you could not do that in Rathlin, I don't think.

> We go to confessions here once a month and mass as well. You would not get time off to do this in Rathlin.

There were many comments of this nature written by the children in St Judes. They seemed to almost regurgitate official church teaching on Catholic education. Indeed this might be the only information they have of Catholic schools *qua* Catholic schools, received, perhaps, from parents or priests. This might explain why in highlighting the difference between Rathlin and themselves their emphases differed from those of their teachers. The latter may well be aware of the less than ideal ethos of Catholic schools. They may also be more aware of the cultural and political connotations attached to Catholic education.

The Protestant children tended to emphasise personality and behavioural differences in their comparisons. While all demonstrated their awareness that St Judes was a Catholic school, this was of less importance to them than was the behaviour of its pupils. This misbehaviour was seen in many cases to be a result of teachers not being strict enough:

> They are disgusting and do the fingers and their teachers don't do anything.

> They are allowed to fight and break windows.

> They smoke and drink and carry on with girlfriends. Their teachers aren't strict enough.

> Other common descriptions used were 'rough', 'bad people',

'dreadful language', 'tough', 'bad words', 'they spit' and 'act badly'.

The only vaguely positive stereotype from all the essays was 'I think they are probably the same as us'!

There was another type of stereotype expressed which, if associated with Catholics in general, is disquieting in the extreme:

St Judes is where all the people that are very bad are sent.

The only ones who go there are ruffians.

And perhaps the most thought-provoking of all:

I don't know anything about St Judes except that they train terrorists there!

From these latter comments of the children, it would seem possible that segregating children of school age may actually institutionalise perceived differences between them and encourage them to formulate antipathetical stereotypes. This may well occur between any neighbouring schools, but in the case of Rathlin and St Judes the differences were seen in terms of each other's religion.

If behaviour may be structured, or at least influenced, by such stereotypes, then the argument that segregated schooling may positively contribute to subsequent community division and conflict is strengthened.

Too often in the past the debate on integrated education has concerned itself with structural problems, and indeed these are daunting enough. However, this chapter would suggest that a much bigger barrier to closer contact between the schools is the attitudinal gulf which exists between the individuals within them.

Even at a pedagogical level there were fundamental differences in rationale between the two groups of teachers. For example, what was perceived by Rathlin staff as responsible behaviour or propriety was seen by teachers in St Judes in terms of rigidity or staidness. Structure and behaviour, therefore, had different meanings for the different individuals. It would seem that these meanings are worthy of much greater consideration than they have been allotted hitherto.

The Catholic teachers' stereotypes appeared to be more outspoken and extreme than did those expressed by Protestant teachers. This concurs with research carried out by O'Donnell (1977). This fact could well be linked to the strong perceived need of Catholics in Northern Ireland to defend the existence of their schools. There are two possible ways of doing this: one can either extol the virtues of the 'Catholic ethos' of such establishments or highlight the shortcomings of the state system and individuals within it. In the absence of any conviction about the former, the teachers in St Judes tended to concentrate their attention on the latter.

Perhaps teachers in state schools, being members of a more generally accepted educational system, felt less compulsion to engage in such 'mud-slinging'.

Finally, one point which may legitimise generalisations to be drawn from the attitudinal data obtained in the two schools. The most common stereotype voiced by St Judes teachers about Rathlin was that it would be rigid and formal, yet the majority of teachers in Rathlin claimed that it was the least formal school in which they had ever taught. Similarly, although the Catholic ('priest-ridden') nature of St Judes was continually emphasised by Rathlin teachers, all of the teachers in St Judes claimed that it would be difficult to find a less Catholic school.

6

An Analysis of Segregation

I HAVE attempted to trace the development of educational segregation in Ireland since the inception of formal primary schooling in 1831 (Chapter 1). An outline of the degree of religious polarisation between schools as it existed in 1977 has also been presented (Chapter 2). Subsequent chapters have concentrated on the similarities and differences between the two sets of schools as they exist today. I have also tried to describe the day-to-day influences and interactions which were experienced by individuals living and working in the separate institutions in an effort to portray what it actually feels like to function in a culturally exclusive establishment.

This chapter attempts the rather more difficult task of analysing the overt manifestations and consequences of separation and grounding the analysis in the broader social context. This pursuit has proved to be the 'graveyard' of many commentators on 'the problem of Northern Ireland'. Nonetheless, my own perceptions and views were so affected during the sojourns with the individuals in both schools that it would be dishonest to do other than give my own appraisal of the situation which is, to a large extent, a consequence of the increased awareness gained in Rathlin and St Judes. My perceptions and assumptions came under greatest assault in Rathlin. This was due (I think) to my possible subscription to a common Catholic view of Protestants in general that they would be grand people if only they would open their minds to the self-evident religious, political and cultural truths of Irish Catholicism! Over the months, the inanity of this view became ever more apparent.

Paradoxically, it may seem that my views have hardened as a result of the experience. They were transformed from those of an avid integrationalist to a position where integration is seen as an option which is rather low on a list of realistic proposals. This is a point to which I will return later.

With regard to this present analysis it should be stated that, in general, approaches to the implications and ramifications of separate schooling in Northern Ireland have been carried out either by apologists of one or other ideological position or by detached outsiders employing questionnaires and surveys which have contributed 'objective' (and I think often misleading) views about segregated schooling. On the other hand, I was afforded the unique opportunity of actually experiencing what it was like to be a participant in *both* types of establishment. Hitherto, no observer has had, or taken, such an opportunity. It is on the basis of this intimate experience that my analysis of social action and reaction proceeds.

The general concepts of character and culture, identity and stereotypes are selected to provide a coherent approach to the multifarious facets of school and community life.

Character and Culture

An essential in any analysis of culture in Northern Ireland is the concept of religion, since the two are so closely related in the province. It is desirable, therefore, to restate briefly the religious composition of both of the schools.

In St Judes every member of staff and all pupils were Catholic. The institution made no claim to be anything other than a Catholic school and it was perceived as such by the entire community. Rathlin had a totally Protestant staff and 99 per cent of its pupils were Protestant. The staff there claimed that, since it was open to all children, it was not correct to describe it as a Protestant school. However, in keeping with all state schools, it was perceived as Protestant by the community which it served.

This difference in religious nature between the two schools may, in itself, account for many of the differences in behaviour between them. In fact it can be argued to represent a central difference. In apologies for Catholic education the claim has consistently been made that salvation of the child is more important than his or her education. Therefore, officially at any rate, religious aspects of schooling are emphasised with academic facets being relegated to a position of secondary importance. Within this rationale, in order to prove itself as 'a good Catholic school', the establishment must demonstrate an effectiveness in the religious domain. This applies particularly at primary level, since it is during this time that Catholic children progress through important 'milestones' (first communion and confession, confirmation, etc.) in their religious development. In keeping with most schools of whatever type, the community tends to know little about what actually takes place within them. Demonstration of religious effectiveness must therefore be made public. Most often this takes the form of announcements at parish mass or of photographs in the local newspapers of the religious aspects of school life.

As a result of the church's official view of education it is hardly surprising that its schools will publicly acclaim their Catholicity more than their educational prowess. Since this Christian objective is presumably non-competitive, the result will be the formation of a distinct collectivity of all Catholic schools, sharing, at least publicly, this common goal.

Rathlin, on the other hand, although Protestant in composition is legally secular. In fact, all religious instruction took place before 9.45 a.m. – that is, outside what was termed the secular day. This practice is common to all state schools. In a society which tends to view education in academic terms it would seem that a state school, in order to demonstrate its success, must emphasise its academic excellence. Rathlin can be seen, therefore, to exist in a more competitive market. The greater its efforts to establish such prestige, the more distinct it becomes as an identifiable entity, i.e. a collectivity distinct, or distinguished, from other state schools.

It must be emphasised that what is being discussed here is the public image of the schools. In this context, comment was often made by teachers in St Judes that Protestant schools were much more publicity conscious than their own. This was demonstrated by more frequent coverage in the newspapers of such events as prize days, open days, debates, sporting achievements, etc. There are two possible reasons which can be proposed to explain this Catholic perception. In the first place, it is true to say that events such as prize days and open days are more popular in state schools (Darby *et al.* 1977), perhaps because they may satisfy the community expectations of state schools. Secondly, as a result of these comments, the press coverage over a period of months was recorded for all primary schools in the area in which the research was carried out. It transpired that the proportion was just about right. However, the vast majority of space attributed to Catholic schools was of a religious nature emphasising a common catholicity.

Perhaps, therefore, the Catholic teachers unconsciously associated such coverage with church rather than school.

It would seem that the public expectations for Catholic schools had the effect of binding all of them together, while those for state schools forced them, through competition, to highlight their differences. This may well explain why examples of ritual in St Judes which emphasised its *character* were rare while in Rathlin they were myriad.

In St Judes, however, the influence of the Catholic philosophy of education was by no means restricted to the public image of the school. In fact much of the school day was taken up by religious matters. The collection of mission money, preparation of hymns for monthly school mass, training of altar boys, prayers and the sacraments were all activities which were considered natural elements of the curriculum. The interesting thing about these activities is that I did not even consider them until observation commenced in Rathlin. There was not one reference in my field notes to such events before this time. It was obvious that, as a Northern Irish Catholic, I had deemed them so natural as not to warrant comment. This note is included here because exactly the same perception seemed to apply to the teachers in St Judes. They claimed that their school was 'not really Catholic' or that 'you could not get a less Catholic school than this one'. These statements seemed to be made in an unconsciousness of significant sections of the school day which were quite specifically Catholic in nature. In other words they were *assumed* to be normal and natural aspects of the curriculum.

This may well explain why the concept of 'Catholic ethos' of schools has consistently proved so elusive and difficult to define. Perhaps, by its very nature, such an ethos is an unconscious phenomenon and, therefore, participants within the schools are unaware of it. In this sense 'ethos' may be most obvious to outside observers and commentators. Certainly the staff in St Judes (and indeed in Rathlin) reacted vociferously against any assertion that their school was in any way special. It might well be, therefore, that for an institution to have an ideal ethos its participants must deem its ramifications and manifestations to be so natural as to be totally unremarkable. This may have the added institutional advantage of precluding self-reflection and, therefore, lessening the possibility of change.

Rathlin, although officially secular, had strong links with various Protestant church groups. Ministers visited the school weekly and were well known to all staff. The school used an adjacent Presbyterian hall for its major public functions. It should also be recalled that the majority of state primary schools, before their transfer to state control in the 1940s, were in fact under the management of the various Protestant denominations. These are still represented at management committee level. Historically, and indeed presently, these interested parties have striven to maintain the Protestant nature of state schools. This interest has implications for the appointment of teachers. Mr McDowell, for example, informed me that he only got his job in his previous school because he had agreed to the 'suggestion' of the local minister to play the organ at Sunday service. However, while Rathlin, and other state schools, are Protestant in composition, they are not homogenously so. The resulting diversity precludes the school from having a unified ethos, at a religious level at least.

Religion *per se* is only one factor in a cultural analysis of Northern Ireland. In fact, some would argue it is incidental. Nonetheless it does determine membership of the major cultural groups and as such it is essential to take cognisance of it. For example, apart altogether from the historic Catholic connection with Nationalism, the fact that Catholicism is emphasised within schools inevitably allies them with Catholic Ireland. In reality this means the Republic of Ireland and ideally, perhaps, a united Ireland. In other words, the emphasis on Catholicism may be seen and, in fact, certainly was seen, as a political acclamation. Thus while the Catholic hierarchy may defend their schools on religious grounds, many Protestants, including the staff in Rathlin, perceived them to be strongly political in nature. Every ritual and symbol observed or heard about in Catholic schools reinforces this perception. This may well explain the antagonism existing against Catholic schools and the reticence of successive Stormont governments to increase financial aid to establishments which were seen to be disloyal and potentially treacherous. It might also explain the comment, expressed by several teachers, that they had been warned that 'no matter how jovial or friendly or free and easy a Catholic might appear, you could (or should) never trust one'. It seemed that Catholicism was perceived as being synonomous with a desire for a united Ireland – an aspiration which represents the ultimate anathema to most Protestants.

Rathlin, being almost totally Protestant in composition, inevitably fostered a Unionist or British culture. The union jack outside the school publicly proclaimed this cultural position. In this respect both schools demonstrated clearly the complex and intricate relationship which exists between religion and culture in Northern Ireland. Catholic staff, observing the cultural symbols exhibited by Rathlin, saw them very much in religious terms. Protestant teachers, commenting on the religious symbols visible in St Judes, equated them with a cultural stance.

Culture is a notoriously difficult concept to define. Tylor (1891) has described it as:

> That complex whole which includes knowledge, beliefs, art, morals, law, custom and any other capabilities and habits acquired by man as a member of society.

Such a comprehensive definition would seem to encompass every facet of human experience and as such make a study of culture in its entirety impossible. I have attempted a cultural analysis of the schools under the basic headings of ritual and symbol. This had two main advantages. Firstly, it allowed a very complex and diffuse area to be studied within manageable parameters. Secondly, it facilitated a consistent approach being employed in both schools. It should not be imagined, however, that the use of such headings implies a clinical approach to culture. In fact, ritual and symbol within the schools were invariably considered in the context of individual action and reaction to them.

The cultural aspects of school life have been considered in other studies, for example Bernstein (1971), Reynolds and Skilbeck (1976). In such studies interest tended to be centred on the effect of cultural demonstrations and transmission on the children attending the schools under scrutiny. In a segregated society such as Northern Ireland, however, there is an even more vital area of concern, i.e. how the cultural rituals and symbols of one type of school system are perceived and reacted to by individuals outside that system. This is of tremendous social significance, since the accusation is often levelled at segregated schools that they not only perpetuate community strife but may actually cause it. Such accusations are normally reinforced with reference to the high degree of polarisation of both staff and pupils in state and maintained schools. It is therefore quite natural, and indeed quite correct, to describe the schools respectively as Protestant and Catholic schools.

The point is that in discussion of the undesirable effects of segregated schooling it is the religious separation of pupils which is most often articulated and postulated as being the cause of community division. However, if religion is the sole criterion used to demonstrate the divisive potential of Northern Irish schools, then how much more pernicious must be the separate churches themselves? If community division is seen exclusively in religious terms then the various churches must be seen to be the most divisive structures in society. Nevertheless, when churches are referred to in debates about community conflict in Northern Ireland the approach is invariably to ask why they are not doing more to stop it, rather than how the separate churches may have caused the conflict. On the other hand, debates about segregated schools carried on in this same context inevitably stress their actual contribution to the perpetuation of violence and conflict. It would seem, therefore, that churches are accorded less positive influence with regard to community conflict than are schools.

One must ask, therefore, what are the aspects of schools which identify them as being the principal 'villains of the piece'. In view of the widespread general interest in segregated schooling it is quite amazing that so little qualitative information is available based on any aspect of schooling other than the formal curriculum.

The findings of my research suggest that at curricular level the schools were almost indistinguishable – the one significant exception being the content of, and approach to, religious instruction. In the Protestant school this was rigidly curtailed to the 'non-secular day', i.e. between 9.00 a.m. and 9.45 a.m. In the Catholic school, however, at certain times of the year religion and religious instruction took preference over all other subjects. For example, the class being prepared for first communion might find two thirds of their day being allotted to this preparation. Preparation of hymns, learning the mass, attending mass and other religious celebrations and daily prayers also took up a significant amount of curricular time.

It is difficult, however, to relate such differing emphases on religion within schools to broader community divisions in Northern Ireland. Different religious groupings proliferate in the province and will continue to do so irrespective of whether schools are segregated or not. No one would deny the right or desirability of such pluralism. It would seem, therefore, that we must consider other factors in any effort to identify specific influences which separate schooling might have on community division.

In this context we must take into account the peculiar position that schools occupy in Northern Ireland, where religion, politics and culture are interwoven to such a significant degree. In general, Protestants subscribe to a Unionist/British ideology and tend to maintain their own cultural traditions, attitudes and values which are largely a function of an English or Scottish identity. Catholics, on the other hand, aspire, to varying degres, towards a Nationalist ideal and possess a set of values and traditions emanating from and identifying with an Irish heritage.

Since it has been demonstrated previously that segregated schools in Northern Ireland can validly be described as either Catholic or Protestant, it is not unreasonable to expect that each type of school will reflect the cultural aspirations of each religious group as a whole. However, the problem with segregated schools, in relation to community divisions, lies not predominantly in the fact that they reflect differing cultures but rather in the meanings which are attributed to the overt demonstrations of these cultural affiliations.

Protestant schools in the North Eastern Library Board area are required to fly the Union Jack outside daily. Individuals within such schools will obviously see this as a natural proclamation for a state school to make. It did, however, provide a general reaction from staff in St Judes:

> They fly the flag down there to show that they are more British than the British themselves. Its also to let us know that they are the lords and masters and we (Catholics) should be continually aware of it.

Again, quite naturally, symbols abound in Catholic schools which emphasise their catholicity (statues, papal flags, crucifixes, etc.). It might be difficult to imagine how these could cause offence. Indeed they can justifiably be seen as a *sine qua non* of Roman Catholic education, which has continually posited salvation higher than education. However, this observation can be transferred into a rather different reality.

One Protestant teacher said:

> We play St Judes often in games and visit their school regularly. I never fail to be impressed by the plethora of religious pictures and

icons staring at you around every corner. It's hard to escape the view that a special show is being put on for our benefit. . . . This doesn't just apply to St Judes of course, but they must know that these are the very things that we object to, yet still they are flaunted everywhere.

These two examples give insight into the gulf which exists between intention and perception in Northern Ireland. The two dominant cultures are so mutually antipathetic that any demonstration of one is perceived as an assault on the other. In this respect, segregated schools stand as public proclamations of the cultural aspirations of each group. But is this necessarily an undesirable aspect of schooling? Surely pluralism *per se* cannot be undesirable in any society. However, in the sensitive state of Northern Ireland, the actual existence of segregated schools has less influence on community divisions than have the meanings which are attributed to them by members of that community.

Hitherto the tendency has been tacitly to accept the detrimental nature of the segregated structures, and debate has proceeded at length at this axiomatic level. However, such structural approaches have offered little with regard to ameliorating divisions in society. Perhaps a phenomenological analysis is more likely to prove fruitful in this context.

Segregated schooling exists uncontentiously in other countries yet fails to do so in Northern Ireland. This would suggest (at least) that the problem lies not within segregated education but rather in the perceptions of the society in which it is operating. In other words, it may well be that it is members of society who have manufactured the controversial identity of segregated schools rather than segregated schooling being *de facto* controversial and divisive. Within this thesis it is likely that some kind of self-fulfilling prophecy may be operating – schools are perceived as divisive and hence become so in their consequences. Perceptions are thus creating reality.

Structuralists would argue of course that if segregated schools were abolished and an integrated system (whatever the phrase is taken to mean) is introduced, then these societal perceptions would disappear. This argument is only tenable, however, if segregated schools can be demonstrated to be *intrinsically* divisive. This has yet to be shown, and indeed in countries other than Northern Ireland seems not to be the case.

Although the two schools did demonstrate differing cultural realities, it is rather difficult to assess the extent to which cultural realities were constructed by the rituals, symbols, messages and cues transmitted within them, or how effective these are in influencing individuals within such organisations. It is in fact doubtful if words such as 'efficiency' should be employed at all in this context. Efficiency implies intent. However, while such stimuli may in fact act to reinforce or create cultural or attitudinal positions, they may also be seen simply as natural affirmations of such positions. In this sense it would seem that the preoccupation of the 'new' sociologists to castigate the consensus of systems theory may in fact be over-emphasising the consciousness aspect of phenomenology. Consciousness seems to have been treated as synonomous with awareness. This is not necessarily so. Teachers in both schools seemed to be conscious of the meanings attached to ritual but demonstrated little awareness of the power or intent of such ritual to influence pupils' attitudes or behaviour. Possibly as a result of this, conscious efforts to influence children seemed to be rarer than traditional and repetitive rituals and behaviour. These may well have had an influence on individuals but were not necessarily perceived by the perpetrators as having this specific, or conscious, function. Individuals, therefore, seemed simply to re-enact ritual not through any conscious conviction but rather through traditional expectation. In the schools it seemed that the transmission and reception of cultural mores and attitudes was, in fact, largely an *unconscious* process.

So far, this section has emphasised the differences between the two schools. There were, however, several factors which resulted in a significant degree of practice common to both. The most influential was the existence of common external academic expectations which are applied to all primary schools and in this context the 'eleven plus' examination provides a common goal for all such schools. As a consequence, the bulk of the action within the schools was identical at the level of formal curriculum. Extra curricular activities also proved rather similar and provided opportunities for contact between the schools through such events as sports, debates, soccer, netball, etc. In fact, it seemed that some of these activities took place more often between Rathlin and St Judes than between the schools of either religious group. It would be a mistake, however, to view such contact or common activities as something which is intrinsically desirable. In the first place, the majority take place in a competetive milieu. Therefore, while these events may seem to represent common values and perhaps a common culture, they may, in fact, serve to accentuate differences rather than similarities between participants. One should remember Mr White's remark when St Judes were playing a Protestant school at soccer – 'There is more to this than just football.' Also, Mr Murphy's claim that he always considered Protestant teams harder to beat and, therefore, took greater pleasure in doing so. It could well be that differences become more important through contact.

It is my view that competitive contact may do more harm than good with regard to relationships between the two sections of the school population. This may arise in no small part from the meanings which are attributed by staff and pupils to such interaction. The fact that St Judes football team donned a Glasgow Celtic strip for all home matches and away matches to other Catholic schools and changed to less emotive attire for away games to Protestant schools, cannot have been overlooked by the pupils of all schools in the league. It would seem that St Judes employed these occasions as opportunities for the acclamation of disparate cultural or value positions rather than to ameliorate the alienating effects of existing structures.

There is nothing remiss, of course, in the demonstration of cultural aspiration or difference, indeed as Bishop Daly (1980) has claimed:

> We should seek a rich unity in diversity rather than a pseudo-conformity which attempts to deny the existence of diversity.

He was, in fact, arguing against the integration of schools and for closer contact taking place between them within the present segregated system of education. He continued:

> The constructive and only realistic way forward is the gradual development of contact between schools of the various traditions and the pupils attending them.

In fact one can easily see the Roman Catholic dilemma in Northern Ireland. The church sees religion as the most important aspect of life. In addition, Catholic education is an essential element in the developement of the child. On the other hand, there exists a Christian awareness of the social implications of separating children at an early age in a province where religious conviction is perceived as a cultural or political statement. Not only this, but the two major cultures tend to be mutually exclusive and antipathetic.

In the light of the Catholic church's conviction of the necessity of a Catholic education and its awareness of the possible social ramifications of such a stance, it is not unreasonable that its bishops should opt for the retention of Catholic schools and recommend increased contact between children. They should also become aware, however, that not all contact is to be recommended and that at the moment the bulk of it may actually be exacerbating friction.

In future, contact between pupils and schools should only be encountenanced if co-operative, rather than competitive, components are emphasised.

Identity

Identity in Northern Ireland, like culture, is a function of religion, politics and history. It is essential to recall that when the state of Northern Ireland was instigated, all legislative structures were constituted and controlled by Protestants. Catholics at the time (1920s) identified more with the Republic of Ireland and to a large extent perceived these structures to be *imposed* upon them. Thus, very basically, Protestants viewed legislatures as protecting their interests. Catholics saw them as impeding their legitimate aspirations. This stark dichotomy has become somewhat clouded in the intervening years, but there still remain strong remnants of these original perceptions.

An interesting, though hardly verifiable, argument can be made that it is religion itself that may determine relative reaction to or identity with governmental structures. Thompson (1970) in his fascinating book on the making on the English working class, cites the early Methodist view of government: 'None shall either in writing or in conversation speak lightly or irreverently of the Government.' On the other hand, the view of the Catholic church has always been that the child is a child first and only secondly a citizen (Fulton 1974). Obviously it would be extremely dubious to base relative identity with government on such tentative (and sparse) information. There is no doubt, however, that there is a marked difference in the extent to which St Judes and Rathlin schools in Northern Ireland accorded authority, and indeed relevance, to the legislative bodies within education (Department of Education,

Education and Library Boards, etc.). This may well be explained by the desparate views of the role of the schools held by church and state.

The state's responsibility is to ensure that its young are to become useful members of society, and its schools are established to serve this function. Rathlin, as part of this system, has, therefore, similar goals to the authorities which control the school. Both the school and state authorities are *united* in this common educational or vocational concern – state and school are mutually reinforcing.

The Catholic church, however, sees education as of secondary importance in the school experience of the young. It is, rather, viewed as an essential experience for the salvation of the soul. This inevitably means that the ultimate authority in schools must be the church rather than the state. Obviously the vocational element of schooling is important in the education of all children. It should also be remembered that the state contributes significantly to the financial upkeep of Catholic schools. Therefore it is legitimate for the state to claim some right of influence in Catholic schools. This would be fine if the demarcation lines between church and state authority were clearly drawn. However, the concept of education in general is notoriously diffuse. Added to this is the Roman Catholic claim that the ethos of their schools should be an 'all pervasive' one, i.e. permeating through the total school experience of children. As a consequence, the church and state have maintained an extremely uneasy relationship with regard to educational control over the years. This institutional tension can hardly be seen in terms of cultural identity, since it obtains in every society where the Catholic church insists on educating its children in its own schools. In Northern Ireland, however, political and historical factors impinge on the situation.

As already discussed, state authority has tended to be Protestant in nature. Education in Northern Ireland should, therefore, be viewed not so much in terms of the more normal church/state debate, but rather as a demonstration of Protestant and Catholic priorities and values; state education serving Protestant demands and Roman Catholic schools catering for Catholic children. Hence the situation exists where state schools relate to state bodies not simply *qua* state bodies but also as reflecting their common Protestant identity. Catholic schools, on the other hand, may lack such a positive identity not merely because of the normal church/state dichotomy but also because of the perceived

Protestant nature of state bodies in Northern Ireland. This negative relationship (for such it seemed to be) of the Catholic school with institutional educational bodies may well reflect the historical lack of empathy of Catholics with broader political structures in the province. In this sense, educational policy-making is perhaps being equated with a political power-base to which Catholics have never subscribed.

Chapter 4 abounds with examples of the differing attitudes of the two schools towards educational authority. All seemed to be encapsulated in two statements made by the principals. Mr Long claimed:

We take for granted the support of the Library Boards whose staff are so helpful when we ask them for their expert advice.

On the other hand, the principal of the Catholic school commented:

I get the children to pay for broken windows themselves. . . it saves me having to get in touch with the Board and have them crawling all over the place.

It is also not without significance that, according to a senior Library Board official, his office received ten times as many enquiries of a trivial nature from state schools as from Catholic schools.

Whatever the reasons for this difference in behaviour within the two schools, the fact that it was observed to prevail in practice may be of significance with regard to community divisions. In this context it would be interesting to determine if other structures of Northern Irish society exist to which Catholics in general, and Catholic schools in particular, attributed similar negative responses. While this aspect of school life was not studied specifically, there were two interesting events in the Catholic school which suggested that negative attitudes were not confined to educational bodies.

The reaction of the majority of St Judes' staff to the visit of the police for a highway code demonstration was far from welcoming. In fact, they described the occasion in terms of showing how liberal the school was in *allowing* the police to visit rather than as what might be considered, in a less polarised society, a quite natural aspect of school life.

It was also observed that pupils in Rathlin paid much more frequent visits to community organisations such as the fire station, local government offices, the post office, police station, etc. When I mentioned this to the staff in St Judes they all agreed that this was probably correct but one claimed:

> What would be the sense in our kids going there? They [as Catholics] will never get a job in a any of them.

What is of interest here is that the Catholic teachers perceived such visits in vocational, rather than civic terms. If this perception is common to the Catholic sector as a whole, and other research evidence by the author cited previously suggest that it is, then it seems inevitable that the two groups will relate to, and identify with, the ordinary, day-to-day structures of their community in entirely different ways.

In general terms, the Catholic teachers were not only curtailing the vocational aspirations of their pupils but also restricting their occupational possibilities. Again, the self-fulfilling prophecy might be operating. If pupils are advised, or given the impression, that they will not get a job in these establishments because of their religion then it is hardly surprising that they become under-represented in these occupational sites.

This rationale, therefore, may well contribute both to perceived and real community differences and divisions. The construction of behaviour based on a perception of division may in fact reify and perpetuate division in the community.

The 'identity' aspect of segregated schooling may, therefore, give cause for concern. It is possible that certain Catholic schools may see their occupational task as preparing children for what they perceive as a discriminatory society. Whether this perception is correct is immaterial. The point is that they can validly be said to be perpetuating community division by directing their pupils to (or away from) certain sections of it.

Stereotypes

The two most striking findings with regard to the stereotypes articulated by individuals in both schools was their unanimity and their almost invariably unfavourable nature. It is also noteworthy that stereotypes expressed tended to be applied to the other cultural group as a whole rather than be confined to educational context, i.e. teachers were seen to behave in a particular way not because they were teachers, but rather because they were either Catholic or Protestant.

It is also important to record that these stereotypes were voiced in a self-confessed ignorance of what actually took place in schools of 'the other sort' and that there appeared to be a degree of mutual suspicion emanating from this lack of first-hand knowledge. What is even more depressing is the possibility that individuals are more inclined to cling to hearsay evidence than to be convinced by more objective information. As one teacher put it, 'Oh, I'm sure there are exceptions, but I'm talking in general terms.' Or another, 'Of course, there are exceptions but I would not be suprised if they acted that way simply because you were there.'

This selective approach to information by teachers is all the more unfortunate as it seems to suggest that these individuals may seek reinforcement for, rather than contradiction of, their traditional attitudinal positions. Since there is little contact between the two systems of schooling, the information readily available to each is the more public, and perhaps superficial, symbols displayed by the separate establishments (flags, statues, publicity, open days, etc.). These are taken by outside observers as vindication of their ill-informed, yet sincerely held, views of what goes within.

This would suggest that there should be more actual contact between state and maintained schools. However, at present such contact tends to take place in a competitive rather than a co-operative milieu and thus may well accentuate differences rather than increase understanding or empathy. Nonetheless, contemporary proposals for the amelioration of the undesirable effects of segregation almost invariably advocate increasing existing contact. This may well be misguided.

At another level, in keeping with other social contexts, contact between schools has been restricted to culturally uncontentious or safe areas. This can be self-defeating. In the first place it is likely to be superficial and thus, as now, simply reinforce existing stereotypes. Secondly, it makes no attempt to come to terms with the very problems for which it is presumably propounded. Contact between schools and schoolchildren must be meaningful. It must encourage rather than avoid confrontation of different attitudes and value positions. The *Schools Cultural Studies Project* has, and is, attempting this but unfortunately has received neither the interest nor acclaim that it deserves.

Strategies such as teacher-exchange, joint community projects and joint cultural/educational trials should be introduced. Concurrent timetabling in adjacent schools (Rathlin and St Judes, for example) might also be implemented. This would facilitate joint classwork, especially in cultural and social studies. Many of these strategies would enable a highlighting of differences and candid discussion and appraisal of different value positions. Consensus need not and should not be the aim, but rather increased awareness, sensitivity and comprehension.

It may seem obvious to claim that it is not segregated schools *per se* that are the problem in Northern Ireland, but rather the meanings and stereotypes which are attributed to them by members of that society. Nevertheless, this aspect is often overlooked in the popular (and facile) structural propositions of integrationalists.

A consideration of stereotypes expressed by teachers and pupils in Rathlin and St Judes provides some reinforcement for the view that segregated schools do, in fact, contribute to community divisions. The whole point about stereotypes is that they are spawned and expressed in ignorance of the subjects about which they are addressed. Indeed it would seem that, almost by definition, ignorance is an essential element in their construction. Separate schooling ensures not only that the children of each major cultural group spend the bulk of their formative years in splendid isolation but also, as a consequence, that they know little about the values, attitudes and aspirations of the other group. What knowledge they do pick up is second-hand in the sense that it is only someone else's account of it. The source is generally as misinformed as the recipient. The result is a little like learning about sex in a school-yard. The statistical likelihood of having a baby as a result of kissing is about the same as being injured by your Catholic or Protesant neighbour! None the less, this latter perception may well be promoted by the fact that many adult Protestants in Northern Ireland have never spoken to a Catholic (and vice versa). Arising from this mutual lack of knowledge comes suspicion and, since most second-hand knowledge is founded on unfavourable stereotypes, fear and reaction lie not too far below the surface.

As stated at the outset of Chapter 5, it is not possible to hold a stereotype of someone or something that we know well. Increased knowledge can only be achieved by frank discussion of value positions held by different individuals. To date the tacit policy throughout society in Northern Ireland has been to avoid the public affirmation of views on contentious issues, perhaps in the naïve hope that they will go away. Unfortunately they haven't.

It seems schools can, and should, provide the setting for social reconstruction. Confrontation of the value positions of pupils and teachers may initially seem an intimidating venture. It is, however, a nettle which can, and must, be grasped.

The bulk of this research was concerned with the social and cultural ramifications of segregated schooling in Northern Ireland. Fieldwork was carried out during a period in which 'the troubles' had prompted a reawakening of interest in the idea of integrating the existing schools there. My experience within the schools has developed a conviction that integrated education is not a feasible proposition in anything but the very remote future. This claim is, in fact, now being expressed more frequently by teachers, academics and Department of Education officials despite the annual (and almost ritual) statistical surveys published by the English 'heavy' press. These invariably purport to demonstrate a significant majority in favour of the integration of schools in Northern Ireland. There are, however, many reasons why the findings of such quantitative approaches should be treated with scepticism. In the first place, as Darby (1977) remarks, 'concern (about segregated schools) does not always extend into an advocacy of integrated schooling'. Secondly, in the emotional arena of Northern Ireland, a person who might normally respond negatively to integration may well not do so lest his response be interpreted as bigotry. Thirdly, this present research and other illuminative studies suggest a strong Protestant perception of integrated education as simply being a case of Catholic schools joining the state system of education. This may well artificially inflate the positive response from that section of the community. It also leads to a fourth *caveat*. Rarely, if ever, in public debate on the subject is the term 'integration' clearly defined, nor indeed is the question of how schools would have to adapt in order to accommodate its implementation discussed. Many of the teachers in both St Judes and Rathlin who had initially expressed themselves in favour of integration became luke-warm when its possible implications for their schools were discussed. One Protestant parent interviewed said he was strongly in favour of integration, but was outraged at my subsequent suggestion that Catholic priests would have right of access!

This present research strongly suggests that, to date, debate for and against integration has been carried on at this naïve and ill-informed level. Perhaps in future more progress might be made if intellect were to guide emotion. Unfortunately, at present, little knowledge exists to inform intellect.

It is precisely this lack of knowledge which contributes most to subsequent community division. The problem lies not so much in segregated schools but rather in a lack of mutual awareness of them. However, stereotypes and attitudes expressed by participants in this study seem to be based on the assumption that segregated schools are inherently divisive. In other words, separateness was seen as synonymous with divisiveness. Added to, and of more importance than, the obvious religious difference, is the fact that one group's cultural treasures tend to be anathema to the other. This was demonstrated in Rathlin and St Judes by the reactions of each school group to the public rituals and symbols displayed by the other.

This, then, is the kernel of the problem of Northern Ireland. At an educational level, in keeping with other sections of society, both sides judge each other across a gulf of ignorance. Arising from this ignorance come the negative responses of suspicion and antipathy. However, study in the schools suggests that there are many positive values and traditions worth retaining and sharing.

Northern Ireland has a rich history and tradition. Children should be encouraged to learn about and from it all, rather than from narrow aspects of selected parts. Observation in St Judes and Rathlin vindicated Gallagher's (1977) claim that at present children on both sides are being denied half of their inheritance.

At the level of religion, Greer (1972), in his research on religious instruction in Northern Irish schools, contends that although Hinduism, Buddhism and other religions are studied in religious education classes, little reference is made to 'the problem of comparative religion which lies at the root of so many social problems in Ireland, the Protestant/Roman Catholic division'. This is indeed so, and provides another example of the futility of a desire for tolerance without the prerequisities of knowledge and comprehension.

With regard to culture, it was manifest that in St Judes and Rathlin two distinct cultures were being fostered. It is essential to recognise these and their distinct indentities and aspirations. It will be futile and misguided to attempt to dilute them in any proposed integration scheme. However, the approach so far with regard to the different cultures in schools has been to play down the fact that they exist. The majority of teachers in St Judes and Rathlin, for example, stated that they avoided 'sensitive issues' in the classroom. However well intentioned this practice may be, it has the unavoidable consequence of perpetuating ignorance of these issues.

O'Neill (1972) has commented on this aspect of life in Northern Ireland:

> We have people genuinely trying to be helpful who advocate a kind of reciprocal emasculation. No national anthem or loyal toast to offend one side; no outward signs or symbols of Nationalism to offend the other. This approach, too, I believe to be misconcieved. It is rather like trying to solve the colour problem by spraying everyone a pale shade of brown.'

Increased knowledge, of course, will not in itself solve the problem. One must take into account the political aspirations which are allied to cultural heritage in Northern Ireland. In fact, especially on the Protestant side, cultural identification may well be seen in terms of the very basic desire for self-preservation. Nonetheless, no progress can be made unless there is a mutual awareness of these aspirations, whether they be cultural or political. At present schools in the province do little to foster such an awareness.

7

Divided We Stand:
The Integration Debate

PERHAPS observations in a small number of schools can best be appreciated by considering them in the broader context of educational systems in other multicultural societies. This is not to suggest that attempts should be make to generalise from case study, but rather that the particular can be consulted in order to better understand the general.

Multicultural societies can be characterised by the existence of a variety of traditions, cultures or religions. The fact that they are not homogenous in tradition or practice may well increase the problems of their members living together. One of the more overt manifestations of such differences is the existence of separate schools. These differences can emerge on the bases of culture, ethnicity, religion or social class. While the latter was not studied specifically, the question of whether separate schools are desirable or harmful features in polycultural societies is raised with regard to the former.

The answer to this question would seem to depend very much on the relationships which exist between the different cultural groups as a whole. For example, a Jewish school in Manchester or Church of England or Catholic schools in London can and do exist uncontentiously. On the other hand, schools for black children in America have tended to cause much more dissension. Separate schools in Eastern Canada are representative of the uneasy relationship existing between 'French' and 'British' Canadians. In Holland, segregated schools have long existed to serve the Catholic and Protestant sections of the population, often disharmoniously.

It would seem, therefore, that since segregated schools can exist in one society without conflict yet fail to do so in another, they cannot be *intrinsically* divisive. It would also appear to reinforce the claim made throughout this book that schools, at a cultural level, tend to reflect differences and conflict rather than cause it. However, many of the arguments used about segregation have been based on the view that they are the cause of division. The natural course of action following from this rationale is to abolish segregated schools and hence, ultimately, eliminate conflict. The enforced bussing of children to and from integrated schools in America is a good example. This demonstrates a conviction that the existing segregated schools are undesirable in themselves.

Two points should be made about segregated schools in America. In the first place, before the enforced integration of schools, there existed a veto against black children enrolling in 'white' schools. No such constraint operates against either cultural group in Northern Ireland, where educational separation is a matter of choice. Secondly, in America there was a question of disparate educational standards between the establishments which added a further dimension to the cultural complexities of segregated schooling there. Nonetheless, it would seem that imposition of integration (or bussing) treats the symptom of a problem rather than its cause.

In Holland, mixed schools were introduced to cater for parents who did not wish to send their children to the existing Catholic or Protestant schools. Although such attendance is in no way imposed, these schools are now considered natural and integral facets of the overall educational system.

Eastern Canada demonstrates a different approach. Here there has been no attempt at integration, and two quite distinct systems of schooling, under the control of two ministers of education, exist for English-speaking and French-speaking children.

In all of these cases the attempts at dealing with multiculturalism at school level have been structural in nature. However, from research in Rathlin and at St Judes, it seems clear that long-term amelioration of the problems associated with separate schooling will only be possible through an appraisal of the attitudes and values which contribute to separation. A consideration of the Jewish school and Church of England school may demonstrate the point. If one were to carry out a participant observation exercise in each of these, it is likely that differences would emerge, many of which would be of the kind recorded in Rathlin and St Judes. Few would argue, however, that an inevitable consequence of this should be some form of integration. In the English context they would not be considered unhealthy or dysfunctional. In this case cultural difference is accepted, or at least tolerated, and the separate schools can foster true pluralism as well as multiculturalism. Perceptions of them are, if not totally supportive, at least not antagonistic.

In a society like Northern Ireland, however, (and this is demonstrated graphically in St Judes and Rathlin) the two major cultures tend to be mutually antipathetic. Overt demonstration in one is interpreted by the other as an attempt to cause offence. It can fairly be argued, therefore, that in Northern Ireland separate schools do tend to perpetuate separatism, but it is the separatism of the uninitiated. In the context of Rathlin and St Judes it seemed that there was rarely an intention to cause affront. Symbols tended to be almost unconcious affirmations of a cultural position.

What should give concern is the misinterpretation of those symbols by outside observers. This is especially so since the segregated schools *themselves* are perceived as symbols of particular religious and cultural positions. It is precisely these perceptions which are likely to make any proposed structural imposition fruitless. Such imposition may actually exacerbate reaction. Instead, the emphasis should be on the creation of a milieu which is receptive to the concept of integration rather than on integration itself. After all, if the former is achieved, the latter becomes largely superfluous.

In addition, attention should be given to the recognition and retention in schools of the very many positive values and aspects of each culture within a society. It is possible that in any proposed (or imposed) integration these may be diluted to what Bishop Daly (1980) has referred to as a 'pseudo-conformity which attempts to deny the existence of diversity'. How then might such a milieu of acceptance be fostered in schools in a society whose major cultures tend to be antipathetic?

In the first place, it should be remembered that in the two schools studied there existed very many aspects of culture which were common to both, such as sport, pop music, television and leisure activities of all kinds. This is likely to obtain in schools in any multicultural society. In fact, it can be argued that there are more cultural features which unite children than which cause division. It is this often overlooked point which may provide the best means for progress. Hitherto contact between segregated schools at the level of common features of culture has tended to be competitive in nature. This has the result of emphasising more global differences. To claim therefore that all contact is desirable is both naïve and misguided.

I propose that two types of contact should be considered between children in the separate schools of any divided society. In the first place there will be the leisure activities which are generally common to all groups. Sport provides a good example of this. Soccer in Holland and Northern Ireland, ice-hockey in Canada and athletics in America all provide common activities for the many diverse cultural groups in those societies. However, great care should be taken in the organisation of contact between schools at this level: Too often they foster an identity with a particular school and, consequently, with the cultural group which it serves. In a competitive context, therefore, such contact may actually accentuate the very differences and division which it was designed to ameliorate. Nonetheless competition is an essential element of almost all sports, and indeed capital can be made of this. Competition should highlight a community identity which would unite children in a cross-cultural motivation. This might simply be achieved by selecting teams to represent a community rather than just one school. Competition could thus mould children in a common goal. Such a procedure would perhaps highlight differences between communities but this is vastly preferable to the accentuation of cultural differences which contribute to conflict in many divided societies. Such a policy would, of course, be of little benefit, and perhaps might even do harm, in societies where conflict arises at a community level – for example, between ghetto areas. However, where division or conflict arises in a society as a result of cultural differences, no opportunity should be lost by educationalists to exploit any 'common ground'.

The second type of contact proposed by this research may be more difficult to implement. A major finding of the work is that the problem of separating children of school age lies not so much with the segregated schools themselves, but rather with the misconceptions, misunderstandings and misinterpretations about each type of establishment held by individuals for whom it was *not* constructed to serve. These arise in no small way from a mutual lack of knowledge, not only of segregated schools but also of the reasons for their existence. The *Schools Apart* (1977) project has also suggested that suspicion results from this lack of awareness.

A truly pluralistic society depends on the tolerance and sensitivity of its members towards the values held by other members. A prerequisite for this, however, is an awareness of these values, since absence of awareness inevitably seems to spawn suspicion, stereotyping and, perhaps, conflict. Superficial contact, as already described, will help to enlighten the children to some extent, but it cannot come to grips with the basic problems of a culturally divided society. This is especially so when the aspirations of one group are anathema to the other. In order for schools to adopt a reconstructionist role, the disparate values and traditions of the children involved must be confronted.

The first step should be that children be made aware of all the value positions which are held by the various groups of the society. This could be done throughout the curriculum, but especially in social studies classes which would be taken by all children. Unfortunately, too often in the past such activities have been perceived as non-academic, non-examinable and, therefore, non-prestigious. The result is that they tend to be offered to 'low ability' classes only. In divided societies, however, curriculum developers must get their priorities right. In these societies, the most basic and most important elements of school curricula must be those that make children aware of the causes of conflict. Such experiences should be presented to children of all abilities. Realistically, perhaps, it can be claimed that the higher ability children will get most out of them and it should also be remembered that it is these children who will become the policy-makers of the future.

Increased awareness, of course, will not in itself solve any problems. In fact, initially it may tend to exacerbate them by merely informing a previously stereotypical bias. As David Kellum (1969) has commented:

> A convinced Nazi who reads the New Testament does not emerge a Christian: he emerges a convinced Nazi now armed with scriptural texts.

In addition to the presentation of information, schools should attempt to foster sensitivity and tolerance among children. There is no doubt, however, that the relativism of acceptance implicit in this tolerance will be difficult for teacher and pupil alike. It is fairly easy to promote a knowledge of someone else's value position but to expect, or demand, acceptance is another matter. The *Schools Cultural Studies* project which has done sterling work in this area in Northern Ireland during the last decade, did, nonetheless, seem to underestimate the un-willingness (or inability) of participants to accept the right to exist of a value position alien to their own. This underestimation applied particularly to teachers.

However, this project did adopt a policy which is worthy of consideration. It included the strategy of values clarification (Raths *et al.*, 1966) which proposes that children attempt to comprehend and clarify values which previously had been held to be axiomatic and absolute. An evaluation (Jenkins *et al.*, 1980) suggests that there is an observable softening of previously extreme value positions among children partaking in the project.

The culmination of such activities should be the confrontation of disparate value positions and, obviously, to achieve this the children from different cultural groups would have to meet together. This highlights the need for contact which is specifically designed to facilitate the confrontation and subsequent amelioration of extreme value positions.

Again this would be a difficult, and perhaps hazardous, procedure but it can be achieved by means of joint timetabling (of, say, social studies) in neighbouring segregated schools. This would enable such activities as joint cultural trails, outings, debates and so on to take place among children of different cultural groups. It would also make possible the very important element of teacher-exchange.

In this chapter I have dealt with the possible procedures which schools serving a divided society might adopt. There is no doubt that many of the extreme attitudes and values of pupils are acquired before they reach school. However, schools seem to do little to redress this fact. The mutual ignorance, antipathy and suspicion demonstrated during this research lend significant support to the claim that schools in divided societies must no longer be content merely to reflect the section of the society which they serve but must rather take upon themselves an active reconstructionist role. If schools fail in this responsibility then the spiral of mutual ignorance, distrust and perhaps violence will continue.

As a result of my experiences in Rathlin, St Judes and other segregated schools in Northern Ireland, I have come to the conclusion that the integration of such schools is an unrealistic proposal. Therefore, at an educational level, attention should be directed towards other strategies which are more likely to soften the extreme attitudes existing among children and adults. This view has been influenced by many factors.

In the first place, there is a prevailing misconception about segregated schools which is most commonly subscribed to by outside observers and commentators. It is the view that the Catholic church represents the single impediment to the introduction of integration. This results in the claim that integration cannot be implemented because of the intransigence of that church. This simply is not the case. It is true to say that Catholics are most outspoken in the defence of the continued existence of their schools. But, as Gallagher (1977) has commented:

> As long as Catholicism has insisted and still insists on its special role in education, so long the rest are absolved any requirement to articulate their position radically.

In this context one should remember the prolonged and intense efforts of the various Protestant churches to 'maintain the Protestant character of the state'. This aspiration still remains strong. The point is that the Catholic church's overt and consistent defence of its own schools removes any obligation from the Protestant churches to 'go public' on their position. There is a further dimension which may give the impression that opposition to integration emanates exclusively from the Catholic 'camp'. Many Protestants perceive integrated education as synonymous with state education, i.e. it is simply a case of Catholic schools joining the state system. Considering the minimal compromise that this would entail for the state (Protestant) system, it is hardly surprising that superficial support is often voiced by members of that sector. In any proposed policy of integration, attempts must be made to accommodate both sets of aspirations and values. Since the overarching tenet of Catholic education is the provision of a Catholic ethos, presumably this requirement would have to be recognised, to some extent at least, in any such proposals. Without exception, when this point was put to Protestant teachers and parents (who initially had voiced their support for integration) they admitted that they would react strongly against such a suggestion. It would seem, therefore, that opposition to the notion of integrated schooling is far from one-sided. In fact, I think it is important to emphasise that a significant majority of parents in Northern Ireland *choose* to have their children educated in segregated schools. It is also important to state that this common opposition to integration stems from religious convictions rather than cultural or social considerations. Again this is often seen by outsiders in terms of intransigence. In fact, it is nothing of the sort.

In England, for example, it would be quite possible and, in fact, relatively easy, to integrate Church of England and Catholic institutions (Roehampton Institute is a case in point). But there the dichotomy is epitomised by religious schools offering an alternative to the relatively 'godless' state establishments. In Northern Ireland, state schools, far from being godless, are strongly Protestant in character. Integration is, therefore, seen as a potential assault on specific religious convictions rather than in terms of the possible general dilution of all religions within a secular system.

This raises another very important point. Although segregated schools in Northern Ireland may offer differing cultural experiences, they are seldom defended for this reason. They exist mainly as a result of religious conviction. On the other hand, the social problems of Northern Ireland stem mainly from cultural and political differences. It would seem to be misguided, therefore, to lay the blame for community divisions at the portals of segregated schools. It has already been argued that segregated schools cannot be intrinsically divisive since they exist without acrimony in other societies. However, in Northern Ireland this religious composition tends to be equated with the distinctive political and cultural differences of the community as a whole. This equation neatly allows the schools to be described in terms of cause rather than effect.

In the context of religious conviction, I think it should be clearly stated that the prevailing educational structures in Northern Ireland are the direct result of each church getting what it wanted. There is a preponderance of both historical and contemporary evidence to support this claim. In reality, state schools serve the needs of Protestant children and Catholic schools satisfy Catholic concerns. There is nothing remiss in this except that it can be claimed to represent an iniquitous situation with regard to the respective financial aid given to each type of establishment. State schools receive 100 per cent grants towards capital expenditure while Catholic schools receive 80 per cent. Of course, it can be argued that Catholic schools have chosen to remain outside the state system and hence cannot expect equality of treatment. This argument is only tenable, however, if the state system of education can be shown to be truly non-denominational. I have claimed throughout that it is not. This is not a criticism, but rather a statement of the reality of segregated schooling in the province. It is important to recall that during the past century the Protestant churches have been just as vociferous in defence of their schools as have Catholics. In fact, after the London-derry Act (1923) the three main Protestant churches claimed that 'the door is now thrown open for a Bolshevist or an atheist or a Roman Catholic to become a teacher in a Protestant *(sic)* school'. I am not sure whether this represented a hierachy of repugnance but it certainly did indicate a strong desire that state schools should be Protestant (or at least non-Catholic) in character. Another indication of this aspiration was given in 1981 when there was a general outcry from the Protestant section of a community whose Education and Library Board appointed two Catholic members to the management committee of a state school. Perhaps Joseph Morgan epitomised a general feeling when he spoke on the floor of Stormont in 1946:

> It is not too much to ask that a Protestant Government elected by a Protestant people should maintain that we should have Protestant teachers for Protestant children.

These examples are restated here in an attempt to demonstrate that today's state schools are as denominational in their own way as are Catholic schools. Perhaps the time is right, therefore, for the British government to offer equal support for Catholic schools. Such a strategy may have the attendant advantage of highlighting the fact that all schools in Northern Ireland serve the same purpose but simply do so in different ways. This pluralistic approach would help to allay the divisive perception which is presently applied to segregated schools. In other words, as distinctiveness is diminished, so also will be the potential for division. There may well be initial opposition to such a proposal; it is nonetheless worthy of serious consideration.

A final basic, yet no less important, aspect of integration is that no one knows, or can agree upon, a meaning of the term. There can be few more infuriating experiences than observing public discussion on the concept of school integration without anyone ever defining the term. Does it mean, for example, that integrated schools would prohibit any overt signs of religious or cultural aspirations? Which (if any) iden-tity would be fostered? Would all clergy be deprived access? Which flags should be flown? Which prayers said? Which games played?

Which songs sung?

Some of these questions may seem banal in the extreme, but they are the realities of separation. Indeed without an appreciation of their importance to the various groups in Northern Ireland we can never hope for increased mutual awareness, sensitivity or tolerance.

The main objective of this book was to increase mutual awareness. The approach was through description and illumination rather than prescription and prediction. Thus no solutions are offered. Ultimately these must come from within the reader rather than from any book. My aim was simply to provide the mirror in which we might view ourselves.

Appendix:
Methodology

The purpose of this section is to describe the methodological procedures employed in the schools in the context of the overall aims and intentions of the research. This process necessarily involves discussion of the bases of comparison between the two schools, and the criteria used in this selection are also enumerated. In addition, I think it is necessary to comment on the difficulties involved in employing the research technique of participant observation and how one can justify such a technique. This justification entails describing the various strategies adopted in the data-gathering process. This is essential for two reasons. In the first place, the strategies can be explained and exemplified in the contexts in which they are being used. Secondly, the reader can better judge the complexities and strengths of the overall work if the basic approaches and research techniques are clearly stated.

I have already commented on the dearth of information existing about Protestant and Catholic schools in Northern Ireland. This lack of knowledge is especially marked at the level of the culture of the schools. Few quantitive and no ethnographic, studies have been carried out in the province. This may seem surprising when one considers the claim often made by educationalists and politicians that the differing experiences of children in their segregated schools contribute to social polarisation and community divisions outside.

The *Schools Apart* project (1977) was an attempt to bridge the gap between the wide general interest in the subject of integrated education in Northern Ireland and the shortage of information about segregated schools.

In common with much sociologically based research the *Schools Apart* project posed as many questions as it answered. This research, therefore, represents a development or refinement of the original project in its attempt to increase our knowledge about segregated schools. It pursues in more depth the general findings of the project. Aspects of school life considered to be especially worthy of further study were:

1. The validity of the claim that Protestant and Catholic schools are significantly different types of institutions.
2. How real are the differences in experiences undergone by Protestant and Catholic children within their separate schools?
3. To what extent do schools reflect or encourage a particular cultural identity?
4. Is this done consciously or, as Skilbeck (1976) would suggest, naïvely?
5. The influence of teachers and others on the structure and character of the school.
6. The influence of church and state on the culture and character of the schools.
7. The influence of perceptions and stereotypes on teacher behaviour.
8. The implications of all of these on possible future integration.

Research Techniques

This section describes the various techniques employed in the collection of data and explains the rationale of adopting such techniques in the light of research aims.

Dale (1972) has commented on the preponderance of sociologies of the classroom and the comparative dearth of sociologies of the staffroom. This study lies predominantly, although not exclusively, in the latter arena. It is not primarily concerned with pedagogy, but rather with the interpretation of teacher action and how that action may subsequently affect the culture and character of the school.

While it was not my original intention to concentrate on the staffroom, I always proposed to focus on teachers. Bruyn (1963), for example, has commented that the researcher needs to participate as fully as possible in the world of his research, learning its languages and attempting to understand negotiations taking place. Becker (1958) claims that any social group will have, to some degree, a culture differing from that of other groups – 'a different set of common understandings around which action is organised'. These differences will find expression in a language whose nuances are peculiar to that group and fully understood only by its members. Blumer (1976) claims that if a researcher wants to understand the action of people it is necessary for him to see objects as they see them. Symbolic interactionalists argue that people act towards objects on the basis of the meaning that these things have for them, not on the basis of the meaning that they have for an outside researcher.

All of these points imply that if the researcher does not make efforts to learn the 'language' of the participants or get to know their 'common understandings' and how they perceive things then his research will have little validity. The six months I spent in each school was barely enough to achieve such learning with teachers alone. Had it included pupils, the learning process could well have taken years!

Even dealing with teachers alone I may always have been seen, albeit to a progressively lesser extent, as 'the researcher'. I had, therefore, to work within this prescribed status and try to come to terms with the constrictions it placed on my activities.

My views on social action and convictions about the importance of the influence of teachers' mediation on the activity within schools had determined that the approach to this research should be both interpretive and participant. I question the view that sociology is a neutral science and that the sociologist should be a neutral observer engaged in purely scientific work.

If the school world is seen in these terms the positivist notions of detachment, distancing and objectivity would seem to be inappropriate methods of studying it. The researcher must actually experience, or 'feel', what the other participants are feeling. These feelings then become legitimate data. Obviously he must always remember that he is a researcher and as such must retain the ability to step back and view the activity not as a participant but rather a researcher. He is, however, not neutral. Neutrality would be self-defeating; it would preclude the very 'feelings' that are the essential data for researchers within the interpretive paradigm. Therefore, objectivity must be seen as a state of balanced emotions rather than an emotional vacuum.

This in itself prompted a participant approach to the research. As the research evolved to focus more specifically on the constructs of character and culture of the schools – which were considered to entail the subjective feelings, attitudes, meanings and aspirations of the participants – it became clear that the researcher should be in a position to share and interpret such meaning structures.

Interpretation of data took place both simultaneously with collection, i.e. in the setting in which they were observed, and also subsequently in the light of data and observations gathered in other settings. An example might best demonstrate the point.

Early on in the observation within St Judes a teacher informed me that he did not say prayers in his classroom because 'it was just brainwash'. Several months later, when I was teaching his class, they refused to leave the classroom at the end of the day 'until they had said their daily prayers'.

It is this type of discrepancy that only the participant can pick up, and indeed this is a significant advantage. However, the more involved the participant aspect, the fewer schools can be studied. In the case of Rathlin and St Judes, therefore, the interpretation must be tentative and analysis cautious. In this context Woods (1977) has commented, 'one case study will not provide the answer to how society operates'. On the other hand, it will not be without worth in this respect. The data obtained are from Northern Irish schools and as such can be compared with data derived from other Northern Irish schools.

Each school was visited initially for four months. Return visits of two months each were subsequently made to the schools to enlarge on areas of particular interest or to check on data gathered during the initial observation. I appreciate that social action within the schools may well be affected by the time of year in which observation took place and that this must be a factor to be considered in any attempts at comparability.

Originally it was my intention to select one or two classrooms and observe almost exclusively in these sites in order to gain some information on the influence that teachers may have on the formation of cultural attitudes and values of the pupils. Quite soon it became apparent that this approach was both impractical and naïve. Long periods passed without any data being collected. All the while I was becoming aware of other potential 'attitude formers' in and around the school; visits of clergy, teacher conversations, artifacts, assemblies ritual – the list was endless.

I decided, therefore, to immerse myself in the total social action of the school rather than be restricted to one or two classrooms.

Concurrent with this shift in research emphasis was a change of physical position. My base became the staffroom and it is the interaction there which forms a significant part of this report. This centre of operations also provided a flow of information about other sites within and outside the school where data could be gathered. Corridors, dining hall, classrooms, toilets, secretary's office and playing fields all became areas where information was checked and rechecked at and from as many sources as possible. The local pub on Fridays or before holidays also provided rich comment on and insight into both schools!

It was considered that the best policy within both schools was to make it clear to the teachers at the outset what I intended to do. Both principals advised me to concentrate on the organisational side of my work and 'play down the Catholic/Protestant bit'! They were obviously concerned that the staff would be alienated initially by the raising of sensitive or uncomfortable issues and thus limit the success of the research. Both principals throughout the time spent in their schools expressed this kind of interest and concern for the research work.

In St Judes the principal explained that he 'had already spoken to the staff about me' and that there was no need for formal introductions or explanations. He reckoned these would be counterproductive – 'My teachers don't like formality, it will only put them off.'

In Rathlin the principal asked me to outline my intentions (underplaying cultural and religious aspects) to the assembled staff at dinner time. He informed his teachers of the event and they all attended. The occasion was a little nerve-racking but served the purpose of initiating conversation with and interest in the 'alien'.

The next priority was to become as much as possible a member of the teaching group. I did this by keeping the same hours they did, taking classes, supervision, games, etc., and eating and drinking with them. I quickly learned to identify and rectify particular aspects of behaviour which emphasised the outsider *persona* of the researcher – passing cigarettes when no one else did, for example. In this same context I quite unashamedly attempted to build up a perceived obligation towards myself from the teachers. I covered their classes, took their duty, marked their essays and gave them the opportunity of getting down to the staffroom for a break. All of these actions built up credits for me as a researcher and indeed the strategy had a solid pay-off in terms of information imparted. On the other hand, the actions did in themselves emphasise the outsider *persona* since no normal teacher would have been so generous!

I may have given the impression of an impersonal approach to the research and the teachers; this was not in fact the case. The first month in each school was spent in getting to know the teachers, in talking, debating, joking and working with them; it was inevitable that friendships developed. Indeed it was such friendships that facilitated entry, as a member, into the social action of the schools.

Unlike Hargreaves (1967) I had no qualms about being identified with teachers within the school. Quite the reverse in fact, since the research was teacher, rather than pupil, orientated; it depended on just such identification. Again, unlike Sharp and Green (1975) who emphasised to staff members that they were not teachers, I, in fact, emphasised that I was, and understood the practical problems which they faced. The implication was that I was not an out-of-touch academic but rather one of themselves.

During this month I made an effort to learn the schedules and geographies of the participants. I drew up lists of activities in both schools which eventually revealed similarities and differences which I subsequently studied in more detail. I made constant checks on factual data and the responses of participants were gathered in as many settings as possible.

Parents, management committee members, clergy and teachers were interviewed in an attempt to obtain as broad a view as possible of the schools.

I anticipated that the interviews with each member of staff could potentially highlight the researcher *persona* more than any other research activity. For this reason this particular methodological approach was the final overt research procedure carried out within both schools. This precaution was graphically vindicated. Word rapidly spread along the grapevine about the sensitive questions which were being asked. Teachers actually were really quite nervous when 'their turn' approached. I was quite taken aback by the anxiety demonstrated by teachers at the outset of each interview. In fact, a significant proportion of the time allocated was given to joking and bantering in an attempt to put them at their ease.

The interviews were structured in the sense that there were discrete areas which I intended to cover – stereotypes, identity, parents, etc. However, respondents were given a large degree of freedom to dwell on areas which were of particular interest to them or about which they had strong opinions or expert knowledge.

The interviews proved to be extremely useful contributions to the understanding of the organisation and culture of the schools in many ways, not least of which was by high-lighting the constellation of views and perceptions of the people within them. Also, by faithfully recording their views I hoped to avoid the criticism that this work was idiosyncratic.

Without exception the respondents overran their projected time allocation of one hour. (One interview lasted two-and-a-half hours!) The teachers, after their initial anxiety, seemed to relish the opportunity of unburdening their feeling and grievances about the school and society.

Four parents from each school were also interviewed. These were selected randomly from the roll book and were seen at home. There was no question of the parents being in any way representative. The interviews themselves were less structured than were those for the teachers and were simply an attempt to elicit points of interest which might be usefully pursued further within the schools. For this reason these parental interviews were carried out in the first month of observation in each school.

Both principals requested that no pupils should be interviewed. They had no objection, however, to the children writing an essay about 'How my school compares with the one nearest to it' (which was, in fact, the other school studied). Such essays were obtained from all P6 and P7 pupils.

It must be emphasised that I was not evaluating the schools but simply working within them in an attempt to make sense of interaction. There were, therefore, no *a priori* theories which required subjection to the logic of falsification. On the other hand, in interpreting the phenomena observed within the schools, I continually drew on my own experience as a teacher and also upon background reading. However, like Best *et al.* (1980) an attempt was made to 'render problematic' not only the assumptions of the teachers within the social context of the schools, but also, as far as possible, my own preconceptions. These latter have been stated throughout so that the reader may judge how far they affect the social action, or emerging hypotheses. Therefore, in anticipating that such hypotheses would emerge from the accounts of individuals, and not simply from my own preconceptions, and accepting that they, in fact, did, I have tried to avoid being accused of hammering reality into shape. In fact, the whole basis of the research was a conviction that it would, as Banks (1977) has claimed for case studies in general, be more valuable for deriving fruitful hypotheses than for testing them.

The approach within the schools, therefore, was strongly influenced by Douglas' (1976) notions of investigative social research. Such methodology includes a good deal of detective work, following up leads and checking out accounts. It involves sifting evidence, and looking out for clues to guide subsequent investigations, and entertaining a healthy scepticism about the accounts that I was given. These may well have been skilfully concocted alibis to conceal the truth. This, of course, involved me in making decisions about facts and truth. Therefore the research is neither totally phenomenological nor relativistic.

The data collected by means of a participant approach must be presented in a form consistent with the way in which the researcher views the construction of social action of the group or institution which is being studied. Much of my time, for example, was spent looking at sources of objective data – roll books, class lists, addresses of pupils, report cards, timetables, notice boards, rotas, textbooks, schedules, etc. These are tangible and important objects which provide insights into school life.

However, the research placed more emphasis on the mediation of individuals on social action and thus on the subjective meaning structures of these individuals acting singly or in groups within the schools. This entailed the observation and recording of their expressed feelings, meaning attributions, reactions and behaviour with regard to the structures and objects existing for them both inside and outside the schools. Information on these aspects is contained in the many field notebooks completed during the research.

An attempt to present all of these would be physically impossible and might carry with it the suggestion that studying them would constitute the same experience as actually constructing them. It is only possible, therefore, to present extracts which are relevant to the aspects of school life, chosen for in-depth study.

This inevitably entailed selection. But, as Walker (1976) claims in his paper on the problems of selection in case study:

> Wastage of information is intrinsic to social research (whether qualitative or quantative), if it were not so, research would hardly

ever be embarked upon. Its (the research) purpose is to make the world more answerable to understanding, not merely to rehearse its complexity.

The third form of data is not available in any tangible form. The actual experience of being present in the research arena for long periods of time gives rise in itself to insights. These experiences are part of the data used in analysis and must be considered essential. Since in many cases data collection and interpretation are concurrent, the interpretation itself becomes important contextual information inseparable from the data.

Criteria for choice of schools

It must be stated at the outset that no claim is made for the two schools selected being representative of other primary schools in Northern Ireland. They are, however, both examples of such such institutions as such are bases for generalisation. I would hope that the information gathered within the schools, and the insights and hypotheses emerging from the data, will serve to increase awareness and understanding of the primary schools which serve both communities in Northern Ireland.

As has already been described, St Jude's and Rathlin were chosen from other schools studied in an earlier research paper (Darby, Murray *et al.,* 1977). The schools were referred to in that report as twinned schools because of their geographic proximity and their good relationships with each other. The schools were sited in a large, mainly Protestant town in Northern Ireland. Relations between all schools in the town are generally good, if somewhat formal, and contact usually takes the form of games, debates, carol services, etc. The Catholic and Protestant primary schools studied are populated by teachers and pupils who represent a broad spectrum of political and social backgrounds.

The principals of both schools were known to me previously and this fact doubtlessly facilitated my entry into the establishments. I had feared beforehand that the nature of the research would be an automatic veto to entry into schools in the sensitive climate of Northern Ireland in 1978. In the event I was given an almost totally free hand to go anywhere and do anything that I wished. The single constraint imposed by both principals was that I should not interview or converse with pupils on sensitive issues.

I knew the staff in St Judes primary school well and was also acquainted with the principal. While this fact no doubt made my entry into the school easier, it also increased the flow of information and comprehension there. In Northern Ireland it is vital that one's background be known so that restrictions on ordinary social interaction can be either imposed or disregarded. In St Judes my credentials were known, and as a Catholic I was obviously considered to be one of them. In other words, at many levels I did not have to work hard in order to gain acceptance.

In Rathlin, my credentials were rapidly researched. One teacher there informed me that several others had been assiduously attempting to discover my first name. Dominic put the issue beyond any doubt! This made my task that much more difficult there, especially since there was a suggestion that I had an interest in matters other than the strictly academic.

In St Judes there was a general acceptance of my research at a cultural level, with perhaps more caution at an academic level. In Rathlin the reverse was rather more the case. Since a significant part of my research was devoted to a study of the culture of the schools, these disparate perceptions of me and my research may well have affected both the flow of information and my comprehension of it within each school. I was well aware of this potential imbalance and have striven throughout to present a fair exposition.

Apart from knowing both principals personally, the two schools were chosen because they seemed to demonstrate a fair degree of comparability. They were both in the same geographical area, were approximately the same size and had exactly the same number of staff. They were, however, distinctly different with regard to their social class structure. According to their principals, Rathlin was 'more middle-class than most' and St Judes 'predominately working-class'. The selection of the schools, therefore, was governed both by academic and pragmatic considerations.

In St Judes there are 410 pupils and a staff of 16 – 6 males (including the principal) and 10 females. It is mainly working-class. Of the 250 children who take dinners, 130 receive them free. The school has an average attendance of 97 per cent and every pupil is Roman Catholic.

Rathlin has an enrolment of 450 pupils and a staff of 16 – 4 male (including the principal and vice-principal) and 12 female. The school is mainly middle-class. Of the 390 children who take school meals daily, 28 receive them free. The school has an average attendance of 96 per cent and it has 6 Catholic children enrolled. The school moved to its present site in 1821.

Problems and Practice

The purpose of this section is to exemplify the already well documented problems of adopting participant observation as a research methodology and to defend such a technique in the context of actual experience within the schools. The section is structured around six headings:

1. Acceptance and Acceptability
2. The Problem of Bracketing
3. The Ethical Problem
4. The Problem of Subjectivity
5. The Problem of Intrusiveness
6. The 'Expert' Researcher

Acceptance and Acceptability

It can be, and indeed has been, argued that it is impossible for a researcher to become totally a member of the participating group. This is accepted, but then no teacher within the schools was, on all occasions, a 'member of the group'. I was included in strictly male conversations in the staffroom when female members of staff were excluded; I was fully accepted into arguments and discussions regarding the infant school when senior school staff were shunned. Across the spectrum of staffroom interaction I was more often included and accepted than any other teacher on the staff, simply because I had the unique ability to change my perceived role and, therefore, avoid being excluded from the action.

A question which caused me much concern was how much I was able or prepared to become fully acceptable. Gans (1968) has commented that the participant observer will always be emotionally first an observer and only secondly a participant. I was aware of this on several occasions. In St Judes the schools football team, who have an awesome reputation, travelled to a nearby village where they were defeated. The teachers who were at the match were enraged and contended that cheating had taken place and they were going to report the teacher from the other school (who had refereed the match) to the central council. I could not experience their outrage, only record it. On another occasion, there was a nasty row in the staffroom about one teacher 'not pulling his weight' – while tempers flared, I clinically observed. Empathy cannot be artificially or rapidly achieved; it may, however, come with time and involvement. On a later occasion, after I had undertaken several training sessions with the football team, I was as disappointed as anyone else when they were defeated in the semi-final of the cup.

At another level, I constantly detected strong antipathy of staff towards the more formal forms of research, coding systems, questionnaires, etc. Therefore, since I was trying to become part of a group which were less than likely to indulge in or appreciate such activities I decided not to employ these instruments. This I hoped would remove the possiblity of my being excluded from the confidence of the group. As one teacher put it, 'It is all right for the type of research you are doing to be funded by the Department of Education because you are seeing what really happens in schools.' He also suggested that teachers would read my research results because they could relate to them as teachers and not be put off by the lists of 'statistical rubbish' that they are usually subjected to. He seemed to be voicing a desire, also stressed by Glaser and Strauss (1968) that research theory should make sense to those to whom the theory applies.

I make no comment on the teacher's views of 'statistical rubbish', but the fact that he did voice them, and that they were greeted with general acclaim, went quite some way in reinforcing my conviction that an interpretive approach was most appropriate.

The Problem of Bracketing

Blumer (1976) has commented:

the entire act of scientific study is orientated and shaped by the underlying picture of the empirical world that is used. This picture sets the selection and formulation, the determination of what are data, the means used in getting data, the kinds of relations sought between data and the forms in which propositions are cast.

One grave danger in adopting a participant and interpretive approach to educational research is that this 'underlying picture of the empirical world' may actually *determine* the data. This possibility might best be demonstrated by anecdote.

I entered St Judes on my first day of observation, timing my arrival to coincide with coffee break. The building had a familiar feel to it, the cheerful bedlam as classrooms disgorged reminded me of the cries of enjoyment from within a public swimming school. Harrassed teachers spilled into the staffroom and, after a cursory appraisal of me, battled forward towards the more important teapot. The teachers that I already knew engaged in friendly baiting of the 'visiting university academic' whom they would soon show the 'right way to do things'. Several were genuinely interested in what I was going to do and discussed how I intended to approach it. They went out of their way to make me feel at home and I rapidly felt at ease.

I arrived at Rathlin for my first full day just after morning class had begun, and passed below a large Union Jack hanging limply on the flagpole outside an ancient, and somewhat intimidating, portal. My steps echoed hollowly on the terrazzo floor as I walked along the old corridors to the empty staffroom. Through each door emanated the almost universal sounds of classroom activity all to the accompaniment of a somewhat cacaphonic rendering of 'God Save the Queen' by some far off recorders. I engaged myself studiously with noticeboards until finally the bell sounded for break.

Classrooms emptied in an orderly fashion. Staff entered carrying large bundles of exercise books which, having procured coffee, they proceeded to mark. Cold suspicious glances were surrepticiously flicked in my direction by solemn-faced staff. The few who did approach me plied me with searching questions on just what I intended to do here. The staffroom seemed very small and I fervently wished I had decided to study chemistry!

It has been argued previously that the attribution of meanings may construct social reality. If this is correct, then certainly on the basis of my feelings on the first day in both schools the reality of St Judes was warm, friendly, humorous and pleasant while Rathlin was cold, suspicious, hostile and intimidating. Quite quickly, however, when I analysed these perceptions, they were seen to be a nonsense.

Goffman (1971) has suggested that the participant researcher must suspend, or 'bracket' his assumptions and preconceptions so that he can step back and look objectively at the social behaviour. My original approach represented the antithesis of such a suggestion. I was judging the Protestant staff through the Northern Irish Catholic's stereotypes of Protestants in general, i.e. cold, humourless, orderly, dour, etc. Since I was expecting these traits in Rathlin school I acted in a more subdued and retiring manner on my first day there. This was, as I discovered later, interpreted as aloofness and I was treated accordingly by the staff. Obviously the opposite applied in St Judes. In the words of Thomas (1928), I was 'perceiving things to be true' and they rapidly became so in their consequences. The social reality of the two staffrooms was constructed not by the main persons involved, but rather the narrow preconceptions of the researcher and some kind of a self-fulfilling prophecy.

At another level, it is difficult for the researcher to bracket assumptions if he is not aware that he is making them. This problem arose many times throughout my research. In the Catholic school in which I started my research I considered many events unworthy of mention; indeed I was hardly aware of their occurrence simply because I, as a Catholic, saw them as normal and natural aspects of school. It was only when I was subsequently researching in a Protestant school that I realised that such events were by no means an essential part of the curriculum. (The suspension or abandoning of classes to prepare for a sung mass at the request of the parish priest is one such example and there are many more cited throughout this report.) Becker (1958) has commented upon the same problem of the researcher missing a lot of what is going on. He sees it in terms of it all being so familiar that it becomes almost impossible to single out events that occur in classrooms, and presumably schools, as things that have occurred even when they happen 'right in front of you'.

For these reasons I returned to both schools for two months to look again with, I hoped, new eyes.

Three possible techniques might be adopted in an attempt to minimise the possibility of missing useful data through accepting phenomena as unremarkable.

1. The researcher should be a total outsider unsullied by any preconceptions of the social system he is about to study.
2. A comparative element should be included in any participant

observation project in order to highlight contrasts in behaviour of the groups concerned.

3. Two researchers should be involved.

The first technique presents many difficulties, not least of which is that it is doubtful if such a person exists. Also, in my case, some of the information which I was seeking (political and religious outlooks, views on teachers of different religions, etc.) would normally, and certainly in Northern Ireland, make it difficult for a complete outsider to succeed.

The second technique has most appeal. The fact that I researched in two different schools, alternating between the two, made me far more aware of the practices in both schools than I would have been had I studied either singly. This was simply because I was able to say, 'Now they did not do it that way in the other school'. It is impossible for a researcher to record all the information about a social system simply by studying that system in isolation. Background reading will help, but cannot be the complete answer. One is almost certain to consider certain actions to be the norm for such systems in general, when in fact they might be quite unique.

There is, however, the danger of the researcher becoming preoccupied with the comparative element to the extent that the wider research ideal is neglected. This possibility was particularly germane to my research since only two schools were involved. In addition, since one was Roman Catholic and the other Protestant, the temptation to generalise, i.e. attribute to Catholicism as a whole that which was observed in the Catholic school, becomes almost unavoidable.

The researcher may well feel, or be made to feel, much more at home in one establishment than in the other. He may thus become much more aware of the hidden feelings and meanings in the former. I was much more apprehensive about entering a state school than the Catholic one with which I had a much closer affinity and better understanding. Being a member of either major religious group in Northern Ireland entails one being privy to a whole set of values, assumptions and traditions not normally accepted, nor indeed understood, by the other group. This factor was particularly apparent in the perceptions section of my work. Catholic teachers were much more open and free in their discussions with me on this topic, quite obviously because they considered me to be one of them. Comments such as 'They [Protestant teachers] would say that, but *you* know that what I am saying is correct', or 'He looks like a typical Protestant', in the total conviction that I would know exactly what they meant (and, unfortunately, I did) were made. I use the word 'unfortunately' because this tacit knowledge was missing in the Protestant school. I was not conversant with the nuances of the 'linguistic fringes' there. On one occasion in the Protestant school two teachers were discussing a parent who had registered his child at the school and had refused to state his religion. They agreed that this was of little consequence since, 'You could tell just by looking at him that he was a Catholic'! The fact that they were correct was interesting, but the fact that I was ignorant of the criteria on which they based their decision and that in this case they couldn't, or wouldn't, explain also highlights one of the difficulties of the comparative approach.

The technique of using two researchers (perhaps in this case, one Protestant and the other Catholic) has some appeal, but problems of consistency may well arise. By its very nature, participant observation necessitates a less structured approach than would be accepted in other research techniques. In fact, it can be argued that it is precisely this lack of structure which enables the researcher to identify and subsequently study events as they arise and not be constrained by predefined instruments. It would be difficult, therefore, for two or more researchers to agree on a uniform approach to their common project if they have no way of predicting what topics will arise in the field.

The Ethical Problem

According to Schutz (1974) every group acts within traditional or handed down norms and basic assumptions and:

> life, especially social life, will continue to be the same as it has been so far; the same problems requiring the same solutions will recur and therefore the former experiences (of the group members) will suffice for mastering future situations. These norms and basic assumptions are not totally private but are likewise accepted and applied by fellow group members.

Schutz, therefore, seems to be painting a picture of a closely knit entity guarding its identity and behaviour by maintaining a code of ethics and conduct wholly known only by the members of the group. Becker (1958) suggests that each group has common understandings and language known only to group members and that social action is organised around these.

In order to acquaint himself fully with these assumptions and ground rules, the participant observer must strive to gain entrance to the group. This entails an overt acceptance of these unwritten rules, otherwise membership will be withheld. It is this aspect of any participant approach which is likely to engender most problems of conscience on the part of the researcher.

My approach within the schools made it difficult for the rest of the staff to see me as anything but a teacher, a fact exemplified by the occasion when the staff suggested that I might be 'spoken to' by the principal for arriving late!

On another occasion a lecturer arrived at Rathlin to observe a student teacher; he took coffee in the staffroom. The two teachers to whom I was talking complained that 'you couldn't talk freely when he was in'. The implication was that he was an intruder while, since the comment was addressed to me, I was not. I constantly and consciously gave the impression that I was, in fact, one of them, and that I accepted and was prepared to defend their assumptions and norms.

The literature on participant observation – (Hargreaves (1967), Jackson (1968), Lacey (1970), Woods *et al.* (1977)) – suggests that if the researcher makes it clear at the outset what he intends to do and how he intends to use any information obtained, this will prevent ethical problems arising. I have reservations about this on several counts. In the first place, if the researcher is totally forthright at the outset it is possible that he will inhibit the participants to such an extent that he is never accepted as one of the group. Even if this doesn't happen, it is quite possible that in the beginning the teachers may see the researcher as an outsider and, as such, as posing no threat as far as confidences are concerned. With constant contact, however, this relationship is bound to change and become less guarded. This, then, is the crux of the ethical problem for the participant observer; on the one hand, he depends on such a change but, on the other, should he take full advantage of it?

A comment often made to me in both schools was, 'I'm only telling you this because I know you so well'. The very essence of such a remark suggests that it prefixed, or was prefixed by, some fact of unusual interest and indeed this was often the case. Also implicit, however, was that there was some confidence involved. In fact, often the most insightful remarks, demonstrating that things were not in fact as they appeared on the surface, were made in the heat of the moment, or in the tacit understanding of the group that they were confidential.

I can propose no easy solution to the ambivalence which any participant observer is almost bound to experience. I could never advocate the 'publish and be damned' approach and anyone who has undertaken participant observation will undertand why. The researcher must always have respect for the group members, many of whom will have become friends. It is in recognition of this friendship, and his responsibility as a researcher, that he should always proceed.

Problem of Subjectivity

By 'subjective' I mean an analysis which focusses upon understandings or conceptualisations of the social world by members within it, as distinct from Smart's (1976) description of 'objective' which refers to the assumed outcomes of interaction, treating these products as entities.

It is often claimed that participant observation is impressionistic, subjective, biased and idiosyncratic. Such claims and counter-claims are well documented (Chanan, Delamont (1976); Woods *et al.* (1977); Travers (1969)) and have already been commented upon in this research. It is possible, however, to argue that subjectivity is *positively advantageous* in educational research. Blumer (1976) argues that if a researcher wants to understand the actions of people it is necessary for him to see objects as they see them:

> People act toward things on the basis of the meaning that these things have for them, not on the basis that they have for an outside observer. This can lead to the setting up of a fictitious world by the researcher.

(See, for example, my first day in both schools.) The stress that is sometimes placed on being objective all too frequently simply results in seeing things from the position of the detached, outside observer. While studying the policy and implications of pupil grouping, I was struck forcibly by the misguidedness of attempting to impose objectivity upon participant accounts and descriptions. In conversation with two individuals who taught two such streamed groups (P7A and P7B in St Judes) I was attempting to find out how much they knew about their respective pupils and their backgrounds. Both were aware of my intentions, and they decided that as a basis for comparison they should use the criterion of how many of the pupil backgrounds they knew 'pretty well'. This entailed knowing 'something about their parents, where they lived and what they did'. No one could ever describe such descriptions as anything but subjective, and indeed I made a futile attempt to impose more rigour upon them. The teachers resisted, however, claiming that they represented appropriate and realistic bases for comparison. One claimed that I would get a truer picture by employing their terms of reference than by imposing mine. In the event the exercise did produce important insights into the constructions and ramifications of ability grouping.

The Problem of Intrusiveness

The question of the obtrusive effect which I, as a researcher, had on the interaction within the schools is difficult to gauge. Parlett and Hamilton (1972) have suggested that the researcher should recognise that his presence might have an effect on the conduct and progress of the research. He should try to be 'unobtrusive without being secretive'. I do not agree. On many occasions I acted as an *agent provocateur* in raising topics which quite often prompted passionate and heated debate. On others I deliberately kept out of debates when the teachers obviously expected me as a member of the group to voice some opinion. It is uncontestable that in both these circumstances I was affecting group behaviour. I contend, however, that while there are many occasions on which the observer can become a 'fly on the wall', there are just as many when he cannot help but be intrusive. This does not necessarily invalidate the research. It may well make group members think about, and discuss, topics which they might not otherwise have done. It is also quite likely that in these circumstances opinions voiced will be 'gut reactions' and not carefully contrived, safe utterances.

This raises the question of whether a phenomenological approach legitimises intrusion. I do not consider it possible for the interpretive researcher to get at 'hidden meanings' by observation alone. In order to achieve any success he must actively probe and chivvy members in a conscious effort to evoke reaction. It is only by studying such reactions in conjunction with passive observation of the group and the constraints upon it that he will be able to make some kind of sense of individual behaviour and the social system as a whole.

The success of participant observation depends on a trust which is continually renegotiated by everyone concerned. On the one hand, the researcher must change from an aloof and obvious outsider (if only as perceived by the group) to a sympathetic, understanding and unremarkable colleague. It is to be hoped that the group members will move from suspicion and perhaps distrust to the openness and acceptance which is vital for the success of the research.

It is rewarding in itself for the researcher to record this build-up of trust, since in everyday relationships one is seldom aware of such a development. It may well increase ethical problems, but the comments that I received from both principals and teachers alike – 'You have made us look at a whole lot of things again' or 'You have done us all good' – suggested that both researcher and participant had gained from the research experience. Bohannan (1978) states that during participant research in schools, both researcher and teacher will (or should) get their culture straight:

> They will discover that much of what had seemed common sense, ordinary background of ordinary social life, about which it had never been necessary to think, is suddenly thrust into prominence and awareness.

This awareness was acutely experienced by me as a researcher and, from their utterances, seems also to have affected the teachers.

Foley (1977) has commented that anthropologists and ethnomethodologists had *ad nauseam* traded on a self image of superior sensitivity and familiarity. Their vague claims seem to have had the effect of either attracting superficial or romantic adoption of their doctrines (participation, interpretation, etc.) or facile rejection on the grounds that their methods are unscientific. Another effect of this 'smugness' is an inability of the educational anthropologists to communicate what they have to offer.

Far from being 'smug', researchers adopting a participant approach must be acutely aware of the potential pitfalls and shortcomings of their chosen methodology.

The Expert Researcher

It is vital to remember the argument of Nell Keddie (1977) that some anthropologists have tended to attribute their own notions of rationality to members' explanations, and thus have prevented these explanations from being tested seriously at face value. An analogy can be drawn between the anthropologist and his primitive group and the educational observer/researcher and teachers and pupils in schools. Within the analogy the researcher tends to see the social action of the school in terms of some kind of academic rationality which, since it is more informed, is by definition a better rationality than that employed by the 'primitive' teachers or pupils in schools (if indeed the latter rationality is considered to exist at all). Thus, as Horton (1977) claims, 'members' accounts must be treated as if they were something else'. One reads in research journals such statements as, 'Teachers gave the impression that. . . but really what they were saying was. . .'

An excerpt from recent literature (Woods (1979)) demonstrates the point. He states:

> often this world (the school life-world) seems composed of an aimless, pointless, disorganised chaos of activity, a childish mucking about or causing trouble through sheer devilment or not paying attention or simply loafing about doing nothing. *However*, it is not as aimless and disorganised as it appears. (My italics.)

Woods then proceeds to argue, cogently, about the function of laughter in schools:

> It is the means by which pupils and teachers displace the grimness, the sourness and hostility that impinges upon them and makes their school lives more palatable, even enjoyable.

Obviously Woods is not prepared to accept explanations that the behaviour is pointless or aimless, since such accounts would be patently nonsense. Therefore, it would seem that he has imposed his meanings on the actions and explanations of the pupils and teachers and, since these actions are now not what they originally seemed to be, they can be explained as serving a social purpose which Horton (1977) would describe as recognisable to the anthropologist (researcher) as reasonable and functional.

This point of view raises serious questions which the participant observer must answer; does defending his *raison d'être* inevitably necessitate the researcher donning the mantle of the 'guru'? In the final analysis is the only true reality that of the informed and enlightened observer? Might this, then, be the real subjectivity 'devil'?

In my own case, it can only be reiterated that there was no question of evaluation, nor *a priori* theories of the action within the schools. I attempted to thrust into prominence that which had seemed the common sense ordinary background of the social life of the schools. My perceptions (and therefore myself) were changed in the process, as, I believe, were those of the participants. If I was tempted to enter the schools as an expert, I most certainly left as a chastened learner.

The description of techniques used in the data-gathering process is included as an appendix in an attempt to demonstrate that the work is neither totally subjective nor idiosyncratic. It is rather a result of constant negotiation of accounts by all of the participants. However, while consultations and discussions formed an integral part of the data itself, the ultimate interpretation of data is mine. My overriding concern throughout has been to present a fair exposition of daily life within the schools.

Bibliography

Akenson, D. H., (1973), *Education and Enmity: The Control of Schooling in Northern Ireland 1920-50,* David and Charles.

Banks, J. A., (1977), *Teaching Strategies for the Social Sciences,* Addison-Wesley.

Barritt, D. P. and Carter, C. F., (1972), *The Northern Ireland Problem: A Sudy in Group relations,* Oxford University Press.

Becker, H. S. (1958), 'Problems in Inference and Proof in Participant Observation', *American Sociological Review,* vol. 23.

Bernstein, B., (1971), 'Education cannot compensate for Society' in B. R. Cosin, I. R. Dale, G. M. Esland and D. F. Swift (eds.), *School and Society: A Sociologial Reader,* Routledge and Kegan Paul.

Best, R. E., Jarvis, C. B. and Ribbins, D., (1980), 'Researching Pastoral Care', *Educational Administration,* vol. 8, no. 1, Winter.

Blumer, H., (1976), 'The Methodological Position of Symbolic Interaction' in M. Hammersley and P. Woods (eds.), *The Process of Schooling,* Routledge and Kegan Paul.

Bohannan, P. J., (1978), 'Field Anthropologists and Classroom Teachers' in A. Hartnett and M. Naish (eds.), *Theory and Practice of Education,* vol. 1. Heinemann.

Boyd, J., (1969), 'Poems Reprinted', *Community Forum,* vol. 4, no. 1.

Bruyn, S., (1963), 'The Methodology of Participant Observation', *Human Organisation,* vol. 22, no. 3.

Campbell, J. J., (1964), *Catholic Schools: A Survey of a Northern Ireland Problem,* Fallons Educational Company.

Commission of Enquiry of the Board of Education in Ireland, (1812) Fourteenth Report.

Conway, Cardinal William, (1971), *Catholic Schools,* Catholic Institute of Ireland.

Cullen, P., (1859), Pastoral Letter. Cited in *Freemans Journal,* Dublin.

Dale , R., (1972), *The Culture of the School,* Open University Press.

Daly, Bishop Cahil, (1978), *The Catholic View of Integrated Education,* unpublished address to the Standing Committee on Segregated Education, Magee College, Londonderry.

Daly, Bishop Edward, (1980), 'Integrated Education', *Network: The Journal of the Association of Teachers of Cultural and Social Studies*, vol. 1, no. 2, December.

Daly, Bishop Edward, (1981), *Integrated Education*, broadcast, Radio Ulster, August.

Darby, J., (1976), *Conflict in Northern Ireland*, Gill & Macmillan.

Darby, J., et al., (1977), *Education and Community in Northern Ireland: Schools Apart?*, New University of Ulster, November.

Delamont, S., (1976), *Interaction in the Classroom*, Methuen.

Douglas, J. D., (1976), *Investigative Social Research*, Sage Publications.

Dowling, P. J., (1971), *A History of Irish Education: A Study in Conflicting Loyalties*, Mercier Press.

Farren, S., (1974), 'Cultural Studies in the Curriculum: A Northern Perspective', *Compass, The Journal of the Irish Association for Curriculum Development*, vol. 3, no. 2.

Farren, S., (1976), 'Culture and Education in Ireland', *Compass, The Journal of the Irish Association for Curriculum Development*, vol. 5, no. 2.

Foley, D. E., (1977), 'Anthropological Studies of Schooling in Developing Countries: Some Recent Trends', *Comparative Educational Review*.

Fulton, J. F., (1973), 'Some Reflections on Catholic Schools in Northern Ireland', in R. Bell, G. Fowler and K. Little (eds.), *Education in Great Britain and Ireland*, Routledge and Kegan Paul.

Gallagher, E., (1977), 'A Protestant Rationale of Segregated Education', paper delivered at Magee College, Londonderry.

Gans, H. J., (1968), 'The Participant Observer as a Human Being', in H. Becker (ed.), *Institutions and the Person*, Aldine.

Glaser, B. G. and Strauss, A. L., (1968), *The Discovery of Grounded Theory*, Weidenfeld & Nicolson.

Goffman, E., (1971), *The Presentation of Self in Everyday Life*, Doubleday.

Gordon, J. E., (1832), 'Six Letters on the Subject of Irish Education', cited in P. J. Dowling, *A History of Irish Education: A Study in Conflicting Loyalties*, Mercier, 1971.

Greer, J., (1972), *A Questioning Society*, Northern Ireland Committee for the Church of Ireland Board of Education.

Greer, J., (1976), 'Religion and Cultural Change', *Compass, The Journal of the Irish Association for Curriculum Development*, vol. 5, no. 2.

Hadkins, L., (1971), 'Irish History Textbooks', *Community Forum*, vol. 1, no. 1.

Hamilton, D., *et al.* (eds.), (1976), *Beyond the Numbers Game: A Reader in Curriculum Evaluation*, Macmillan.

Hargreaves, D. H., (1967), *Social Relations in a Secondary School*, Routledge & Kegan Paul.

Heskin, K., (1980), *Northern Ireland : A Psychological Analysis*, Gill & Macmillan.

Jackson, P. W., (1968), *Life in Classrooms*, Holt, Rinehart & Winston.

Jenkins, D. and O'Connor, S., (1980), *Chocolate Cream Soldiers*, evaluation report on the Schools Cultural Studies Project, New University of Ulster.

Keddie, N. G., (1977), 'Education as a Social Construct' in C. Jenks (ed.), *Rationality, Education and the Social Organisation of Knowledge*, Routledge & Kegan Paul.

Kellum, D., (1969), *The Social Studies: Myths and Reality*, Sheed & Ward.

Lacey, C., (1970), *Hightown Grammar*, Manchester University Press.

Magee, J., (1970), 'The Teaching of Irish History in Irish Schools', *The Northern Teacher*, vol. 10, no. 1, Winter.

Magee, J., (1974), *Northern Ireland – Crisis and Conflict*, Routledge & Kegan Paul.

March, J., (ed.), (1965), *Handbook of Organisation*, Rand McNally.

Morgan, J., (1964), Speech to Stormont Parliament, cited in J. J. Campbell, *Catholic Schools*, Fallons.

Morrison, H., (1923), Speech to Stormont Parliament, cited in D. H. Akenson, *Education and Emnity*, David & Charles.

Murray, D., (1978), 'Education and Community in Northern Ireland', *Northern Teacher*, vol. 13, no. 2, Summer.

Murray, D., (1979a), 'Schools and Identity in Northern Ireland', Internal report for the Schools Cultural Studies Project, February 1979.

Murray, D., (1979b), 'Attitudes and Stereotypes of School children in Northern Irish Schools', *Report to the Northern Ireland Department of Education* (unpublished).

Murray, D., (1980a), 'Values Clarification in Cultural Studies', Paper read at the conference of the Association of Teachers of Social Studies, Liverpool, September, 1980.

Murray, D., (1980b), 'Joint Work: A Tool for Reconstruction', *Network, The Journal of the Association of teachers of Cultural and Social Studies*, vol. 1, no. 2, December.

Murray, D., (1983), *A Comparative Study of the Culture and Character of Protestant and Catholic Primary Schools in Northern Ireland*, unpublished D. Phil. Thesis, New University of Ulster.

McCloskey, N. G., (1962), *The Catholic Viewpoint in Education*, Doubleday Books.

O'Donnell, E, (1977), *Northern Irish Stereotypes*, Redwood Burn Ltd.

O'Fiaich, Cardinal T., (1979), 'The Atmosphere of the Catholic School', *Irish News*, November.

O'Neill, T., (1972), *An Autobiography*, Hart-Davis.

Philbin, Bishop W., (1975), *Pastoral Letter*, Down and Connor, Easter.

Raths, L., Harmin, M. and Simon, S, (1966), *Values and Teaching*, Merril.

Robinson, A., (1971), 'Education and Sectarian Conflict in Northern Ireland', *New Era* , vol. 52, no. 1, January.

Robinson, A., (1980), 'Social Studies in Northern Ireland: The Schools Cultural Studies Project', *The Social Studies Teacher*, vol. 9, no. 3, February.

Rogers, W. R., (1947), 'Poems Reprinted', *Community Forum*, vol. 4, no. 1.

Russell, J., (1972), 'Some Aspects of the Civic Education of Secondary Schoolboys in Northern Ireland', *Northern Ireland Community Relations Commission*, research paper.

Schools Cultural Studies Project, (1981), 'A contribution to the further development of culture in Northern Ireland', Directors report submitted to sponsoring bodies, Joseph Rowentree Charitable Trust, Northern Ireland Department of Education, New University of Ulster.

Schutz, A., (1974), 'The Stranger: An essay in Social Psychology' in B. R. Cosin, I. R. Dale, G. M. Esland and D. F. Swift (eds.), *School and Society: A Sociological Reader*, Routledge & Kegan Paul.

Sharp, R. and Green, A., (1975), *Education and Social Control: A Study in Progressive Primary Education*, Routledge and Kegan Paul.

Skilbeck, M, (1973), 'The School and Cultural Development', *The Northern Teacher,* Winter.

Skilbeck, M., (1973b), 'Schools and Culture in Northern Ireland', unpublished paper for the Schools Cultural Studies Project. New University of Ulster.

Skilbeck, M., (1976), 'Education and Cultural Change', *Compass, Journal of the Irish Association for Curriculum Development,* vol. 5, no. 2.

Socket, H., (1979), 'A Review of Chocolate Cream Soldiers', a reply to the evaluation report on the Schools Cultural Studies Project, New University of Ulster.

Spencer, T., (1974), Comments to a meeting of the Belfast Education and Library Board, citied in *Education Times,* February.

Sutherland, M., (1973), 'Education in Northern Ireland' in R. Bell, G. and K. Little, *Education in Great Britain and Ireland: A Source Book,* Routledge & Kegan Paul for the Open University.

Thomas, W. I., (1928), *The Child in America,* Knopf.

Thompson, E. P., (1970), *The Making of the English Working Class,* Penguin.

Travers, R. M. W., (1969), *An Introduction to Educational Research,* Macmillan.

Tylor, E. B., (1871), *Primitive Culture,* London.

Van Der Plas, (1967), *Those Dutch Catholics,* Chapman.

Walker, R., (1976), 'Making Sense and Losing Meaning: Problems of Selection in Doing Case Study', *Care,* October.

Winning, Archbishop, (1976), *Pastoral Letter,* Glasgow.

Woods, P., (1979), *The Divided School,* Routledge & Kegan Paul.

Woods, P. E. and Hammersley, M., (eds.), (1977), *School Experience,* Croom Helm.

Index